# AMONG THE NIGHT PEOPLE

COLLIE CHASED HIM AWAY.

# AMONG THE NIGHT PEOPLE

BY

## CLARA DILLINGHAM PIERSON

**Author of "Among the Meadow People," "Pond People," etc.**

## YESTERDAY'S CLASSICS

### CHAPEL HILL, NORTH CAROLINA

This edition, first published in 2005 by Yesterday's Classics, is an unabridged republication of the work originally published by E. P. Dutton and Company in 1902. The color illustrations by F. C. Gordon in that volume are rendered in black and white in this edition. For a listing of books published by Yesterday's Classics, visit www.yesterdaysclassics.com. Yesterday's Classics is the publishing arm of the Baldwin Project which presents the complete text of dozens of classic books for children at www.mainlesson.com under the editorship of Lisa M. Ripperton and T. A. Roth.

ISBN-10:   1-59915-020-4

ISBN-13:   978-1-59915-020-8


Yesterday's Classics
PO Box 3418
Chapel Hill, NC 27515

TO

# RACHEL W. PIERSON

**THIS BOOK IS AFFECTIONATELY DEDICATED**

# CONTENTS

My Dear Little Friends:—You can never guess how much I have enjoyed writing these stories of the night-time, and I must tell you how I first came to think of doing so. I once knew a girl—and she was not a very little girl, either,—who was afraid of the dark. And I have known three boys who were as brave as could be by daylight, but who would not run on an errand alone after the lamps were lighted. They never seemed to think what a beautiful, restful, growing time the night is for plants and animals, and even for themselves. I thought that if they knew more of what happens between sunset and sunrise they would love the night as well as I.

It may be that you will never see Bats flying freely, or find the Owls flapping silently among the trees without touching even a twig. Perhaps while these things are happening you must be snugly tucked in bed. But that is no reason why you should not be told what they do while you are dreaming. Before this, you know, I have told you more of what is done by daylight in meadow, forest, farmyard, and pond. It would be a very queer world if we could not know about things without seeing them for ourselves, and you may like to think, when you are going to sleep, that hundreds and thousands of tiny out-of-door people are turning, and stretching, and going to find their food. In the morning, when you are dressing in your sunshiny rooms, they are cuddling down for a good day's rest.

I think I ought to tell you that I have not been alone when writing these stories. I have often been in the meadow and the forest at night, and have seen and heard many interesting things, but my good Cat, Silvertip, has known far more than I of the night-doings of the out-of-door people. He has been beside me at my desk, and although at times he has shut his eyes and taken Cat-naps while I wrote, there have been many other times when he has taken the pen right out of my hand. He has even tried running the typewriter with his dainty white paws, and he has gone over every story that I have written. I do not say that he has written any himself, but you can see that he has been very careful what I wrote, and I have learned a great deal from him that I never knew before. He is a very good and clever Cat, and if you like these stories I am sure it must be partly because he had a paw in the writing of them.

Your friend,

CLARA D. PIERSON.

STANTON, MICHIGAN,
  April 15th, 1901.

# THE BLACK SPANISH CHICKENS

WHEN the Speckled Hen wanted to sit there was no use in trying to talk her out of the idea, for she was a very set Hen. So, after the farmer's wife had worked and worked, and barred her out of first one nesting-place and then another, she gave up to the Speckled Hen and fixed her a fine nest and put thirteen eggs into it. They were Black Spanish eggs, but the Speckled Hen did not know that. The Hens that had laid them could not bear to sit, so, unless some other Hen did the work which they left undone, there would have been no Black Spanish Chickens. This is always their way, and people have grown used to it. Now nobody thinks of asking a Black Spanish Hen to sit, although it does not seem right that a Hen should be unwilling to bring up chickens. Supposing nobody had been willing to bring her up?

Still, the Black Spanish Hens talk very reasonably about it. "We will lay plenty of eggs," they say, "but some of the common Hens must hatch them." They do their share of the farmyard

1

work, only they insist on choosing what that share shall be.

When the Speckled Hen came off the nest with eleven Black Chickens (two of the eggs did not hatch), she was not altogether happy. "I wanted them to be speckled," said she, "and not one of the whole brood is." That was why she grew so restless and discontented in her coop, although it was roomy and clean and she had plenty given her to eat and drink. She was quite happy only when they were safely under her wings at night. And such a time as they always had getting settled!

When the sunbeams came more and more slantingly through the trees, the Chickens felt less and less like running around. Their tiny legs were tired and they liked to cuddle down on the grass in the shadow of the coop. Then the Speckled Hen often clucked to them to come in and rest, but they liked it better in the open air. The Speckled Hen would also have liked to be out of the coop, yet the farmer kept her in. He knew what was best for Hens with little Chickens, and also what was best for the tender young lettuce and radishes in his garden.

When the sun was nearly down, the Speckled Hen clucked her come-to-bed cluck, which was quite different from her food cluck or her Hawk cluck, and the little Black Chickens ran between the bars and crawled under her feathers. Then the Speckled Hen began to look fatter and fatter and fatter for each Chicken who nestled beneath her. Sometimes one little fellow would scramble up on to her back and stand there, while she turned her head from side to side, looking at him with first one and then the other of her round yellow eyes, and scolding him all the time. It never did any good to scold, but she said she had to do something, and with ten other children under her wings it would never do for her to stand up and tumble him off.

All the time that they were getting settled for the night the Chickens were talking in sleepy little cheeps, and now and then one of them would poke his head out between the feathers and tell the Speckled Hen that somebody was pushing him. Then she would be more puzzled than ever and cluck louder still. Sometimes, too, the Chickens would run out for another mouthful of cornmeal mush or a few more drops of water. There was one little fellow who always wanted something to drink just when he should have been going to sleep. The Speckled Hen used to say that it took longer for a mouthful of water to run down his throat than it would for her to drink the whole panful. Of course it did take quite a while, because he couldn't hurry it by swallowing. He had to drink, as all birds do, by filling his beak with water and then holding it up until the last drop had trickled down into his stomach.

When the whole eleven were at last safely tucked away for the night, the Speckled Hen was tired but happy. "They are good children," she often said to herself, "if they are Black Spanish. They might be just as mischievous if they were speckled; still, I do wish that those stylish-looking, white-eared Black Spanish Hens would raise their own broods. I

3

don't like to be hatch-mother to other Hens' chickens." Then she would slide her eyelids over her eyes, and doze off, and dream that they were all speckled like herself.

There came a day when the coop was raised and they were free to go where they chose. There was a fence around the vegetable garden now and netting around the flower-beds, but there were other lovely places for scratching up food, for nipping off tender young green things, for picking up the fine gravel which every Chicken needs, and for wallowing in the dust. Then the Black Spanish Chickens became acquainted with the other fowls whom they had never met before. They were rather afraid of the Shanghai Cock because he had such a gruff way of speaking, and they liked the Dorkings, yet the ones they watched and admired and talked most about were the Black Spanish Cock and Hen. There were many fowls on the farm who did not have family names, and the Speckled Hen was one of these. They had been there longer than the rest and did not really like having new people come to live in the poultry-yard. It was trying, too, when the older Hens had to hatch the eggs laid by the newcomers.

It is said that this was what made the Speckled Hen leave the eleven little Black Spanish Chickens after she had been out of the coop for a while. They had been very mischievous and disobedient one day, and she walked off and left them to care for themselves while she started to raise a family of her own in a stolen nest under the straw-stack.

THEY WERE FREE TO GO WHERE THEY CHOSE.

When night came, eleven little Black Spanish Chickens did not know what to do. They went to look for their old coop, but that had been given to another Hen and her family. They walked around looking very small and lonely, and wished they had minded the Speckled Hen and made her love them more. At last they found an old potato-crate which reminded them of a coop and so seemed rather homelike. It stood, top down, upon the ground and they were too big to crawl through its barred sides, so they did the best they could and huddled together on top of it. If there had not been a stone-heap near, they could not have done that, for their wing-feathers were not yet large enough to help them flutter. The bravest Chicken went first, picking his way from stone to stone until he reached the highest one, balancing himself awhile on that, stretching his neck toward the potato-crate, looking at it as though he were about to jump, and then seeming to change his mind and decide not to do so after all.

The Chickens on the ground said he was afraid, and he said he wasn't any more afraid than they were. Then, after a while, he did jump, a queer, floppy, squawky kind of jump, but it landed him where he wanted to be. After that it was his turn to laugh at the others while they stood teetering uncertainly on the top stone. They were very lonely without the Speckled Hen, and each Chicken wanted to be in the middle of the group to keep him warm on all sides.

Somebody laughed at the most mischievous Chicken and told him he could stand on the potato-crate's back without being scolded, and he pouted his bill and said: "Much fun that would be! All I cared about standing on the Speckled Hen's back was to make her scold!" It is very shocking that he should say such things, but he did say exactly that.

They slept safely that night, and only awakened when the Cocks crowed a little while after midnight. After that they slept until sunrise, and when the Shanghais and Dorkings came down from the apple-tree where they had been roosting, the Black Spanish Chickens stirred and cheeped, and looked at their feathers to see how much they had grown during the night. Then they pushed and squabbled for their breakfast.

Every night they came back to sleep on the potato-crate. At last they were able to spring up into their places without standing on the stone-pile, and that was a great day. They talked about it long after they should have been asleep, and were still chattering when the Shanghai Cock spoke: "If you Black Spanish Chickens don't keep still and let us sleep," said he, "some Owl or Weasel will come for you, and I shall be glad to have him!"

That scared the Chickens and they were very quiet. It made the Black Spanish Hen uneasy though, and she whispered to the Black Spanish Cock and wouldn't let him sleep until he had promised to fight anybody who might try to carry one of the Chickens away from the potato-crate.

The next night first one Chicken and then another kept tumbling off the potato-crate. They lost their patience and said such things as these to each other:

"You pushed me! You know you did!"

"Well, he pushed me!"

"Didn't either!"

"Did too!"

"Well, I couldn't help it if I did!"

The Shanghai Cock became exceedingly cross because they made so much noise, and even the Black Spanish Cock lost his patience. "You may be my children," said he, "but you do not take your manners from me. Is there no other place on this farm where you can sleep excepting that old crate?"

"We want to sleep here," answered the Chicken on the ground. "There is plenty of room if those fellows wouldn't push." Then he flew up and clung and pushed until some other Chicken tumbled off.

"Well!" said the Black Spanish Cock. And he would have said much more if the Black Spanish Hen had not fluttered down from the apple-tree to see what was the matter. When he saw the expression of her eyes he decided to go back to his perch.

"There is not room for you all," said the Black Spanish Hen. "One must sleep somewhere else."

"There *is* room," said the Chickens, contradicting her. "We have always roosted on here."

"There is *not* room," said the Black Spanish Hen once more. "How do your feathers grow?"

"Finely," said they.

"And your feet?"

"They are getting very big," was the answer.

"Do you think the Speckled Hen could cover you all with her wings if she were to try it now?"

The Chickens looked at each other and laughed. They thought it would take three Speckled Hens to cover them.

"But she used to," said the Black Spanish Hen. She did not say anything more. She just looked at the potato-crate and at them and at the potato-crate again. Then she walked off.

After a while one of the Chickens said: "I guess perhaps there isn't room for us all there."

The mischievous one said: "If you little Chickens want to roost there you may. I am too large for that sort of thing." Then he walked up the slanting board to the apple-tree branch and perched there beside the young Shanghais. You should have seen how beautifully he did it. His toes hooked themselves around the branch as though he had always perched there, and he tucked his head under his wing with quite an air. Before long his brothers and sisters came also, and heard him saying to one of his new neighbors, "Oh, yes, I much prefer apple-trees, but when I was a Chicken I used to sleep on a potato-crate."

9

"Just listen to him!" whispered the Black Spanish Cock. "And he hasn't a tail-feather worth mentioning!"

"Never mind," answered the Black Spanish Hen. "Let them play that they are grown up if they want to. They will be soon enough." She sighed as she put her head under her wing and settled down for the night. It made her feel old to see her children roosting in a tree.

# THE WIGGLERS BECOME MOSQUITOES

IT was a bright moonlight night when the oldest Wigglers in the rain-barrel made up their mind to leave the water. They had always been restless and discontented children, but it was not altogether their fault. How could one expect any insect with such a name to float quietly? When the Mosquito Mothers laid their long and slender eggs in the rain-barrel, they had fastened them together in boat-shaped masses, and there they had floated until the Wigglers were strong enough to break through the lower ends of the eggs into the water. It had been only a few days before they were ready to do this.

Then there had been a few more days and nights when the tiny Wigglers hung head downward in the water, and all one could see by looking across the barrel was the tips of their breathing tubes. Sometimes, if they were frightened, a young Wiggler would forget and get head uppermost for a minute, but he was always ashamed to have this happen, and made all sorts of excuses for himself when it did. Well-bred little Wigglers tried to always have their heads down, and Mosquitoes who stopped to visit with them and give good advice told them such things as these: "The Wiggler who keeps his head up may never have wings," and, "Up with your tails and down with your eyes, if you would be mannerly, healthy, and wise."

When they were very young they kept their heads way down and breathed through a tube that ran out near the tail-end of their bodies. This tube had a cluster of tiny wing-like things on the very tip, which kept it floating on the top of the water. They had no work to do, so they just ate food which they found in the water, and wiggled, and played tag, and whenever they were at all frightened they dived to the bottom and stayed there until they were out of breath. That was never very long.

There were many things to frighten them. Sometimes a stray Horse stopped by the barrel to drink, sometimes a Robin perched on the edge for a few mouthfuls of water, and once in a while a Dragon-Fly came over to visit from the neighboring pond. It was not always the biggest visitor who scared them the worst. The Horses tried not to touch the Wigglers, while a Robin was only too glad if he happened to get one into his bill with the water. The Dragon-Flies were the worst, for they were the hungriest, and they were so much smaller that sometimes the Wigglers didn't see them coming. Sometimes, too, when they thought that a Dragon-Fly was going the other way, some of them stayed near the top of the water, only to find when it was too late that a Dragon-Fly can go backwards or sidewise without turning around.

When they were a few days old the Wigglers began to change their skins. This they did by wiggling out of their old ones and wearing the new ones which had been growing underneath. This made them feel exceedingly important, and some of them became disgracefully vain. One Wiggler would not dive until he was sure a certain Robin had seen his new suit. It was because of that vanity he never lived to be a Mosquito.

After they had changed their skins a few times, they had two breathing-tubes apiece instead of one, and these two grew out near their heads. And their heads were much larger. At the tail-end of his body each Wiggler now had two leaf-like things with which he swam through the water. Because they used different breathing-tubes, those Wigglers who had moulted or cast their skins several times now floated in the water with their heads just below the surface and their tails down. When a Wiggler is old enough for this, he is called a Pupa, or half-grown one.

There are often young Mosquito children of all ages in the same barrel—eggs, Wigglers, and Pupæ all together. There is plenty of room and plenty of food, but because they have no work to do there is much time for quarrelling and talking about each other.

This year the Oldest Brother had put on so many airs that nobody liked it at all, and several of the Wigglers had been heard to say that they couldn't bear the sight of him. He had such a way of saying, "When I was a young Wiggler and had to keep my head down," or repeating, "Up with your tails and down with your eyes, if you would be mannerly, healthy, and wise." One little Wiggler crossed his feelers at him, and they say that it is just as bad to do that as to make faces. Besides, it is so much easier— if you have the feelers to cross.

Now the Oldest Brother and those of his brothers and sisters who had hatched from the same egg-mass were talking of leaving the rain-barrel forever. It was a bright moonlight night and they longed to get their wings uncovered and dried, for then they would be full-grown Mosquitoes, resting most of the day and having glorious times at night.

The Oldest Brother was jerking himself through the water as fast as he could, giving his jointed body sudden bends, first this way and then that, and when he met any one nearly his own age he said, "Come with me and cast your skin. It is a fine evening for moulting."

Sometimes they answered, "All right," and jerked or wiggled or swam along with him, and sometimes a Pupa would answer, "I'm afraid I'm not old enough to slip out of my skin easily."

Then the Oldest Brother would reply, "Don't stop for that. You'll be older by the time we begin." That was true, of course, and all members of Mosquito families grow old very fast. So it happened that when the moon peeped over the farmhouse, showing her bright face between the two chimneys, twenty-three Pupæ were floating close to each other and making ready to change their skins for the last time.

It was very exciting. All the young Wigglers hung around to see what was going on, and pushed each other aside to get the best places. The Oldest Brother was much afraid that somebody else would begin to moult before he was ready, and all the brothers were telling their sisters to be careful to split their skins in the right place down the back, and the sisters were telling them that they knew just as much about moulting as their brothers did. Every little while the Oldest Brother would say, "Now wait! Don't one of you fellows split his old skin until I say so."

Then two or three of his brothers would become impatient, because their outer skins were growing tighter every minute, and would say, "Why not?" and would grumble because they had to wait. The truth was that the Oldest Brother could not get his skin to crack, although he jerked and wiggled and took very deep breaths. And he didn't want any one else to get ahead of him. At last it did begin to open, and he had just told the others to commence moulting, when a Mosquito Mother stopped to lay a few eggs in the barrel.

"Dear me!" said she. "You are not going to moult to-night, are you?"

"Yes, we are," answered the Oldest Brother, giving a wiggle that split his skin a little farther. "We'll be biting people before morning."

"You?" said the Mosquito Mother, with a queer little smile. "I wouldn't count on doing that. But you young people may get into trouble if you moult now, for it looks like rain."

She waved her feelers upward as she spoke, and they noticed that heavy black clouds were piling up in the sky. Even as they looked the moon was hidden and the wind began to stir the branches of the trees. "It will rain," she said, "and then the water will run off the roof into this barrel, and if you have just moulted and cannot fly, you will be drowned."

"Pooh!" answered the Oldest Brother. "Guess we can take care of ourselves. I'm not afraid of a little water." Then he tried to crawl out of his old skin.

The Mosquito Mother stayed until she had laid all the eggs she wanted to, and then flew away. Not one of the Pupæ had been willing to listen to her, although some of the sisters might have done so if their brothers had not made fun of them.

At last, twenty-three soft and tired young Mosquitoes stood on their cast-off pupa-skins, waiting for their wings to harden. It is never easy work to crawl out of one's skin, and the last moulting is the hardest of all. It was then, when they could do nothing but wait, that these young Mosquitoes began to feel afraid. The night was now dark and windy, and sometimes a sudden gust blew their floating pupa-skins toward one side of the barrel. They had to cling tightly to them, for they suddenly remembered that if they fell into the water they might drown. The oldest one found himself wishing to be a Wiggler again. "Wigglers are never drowned," thought he.

"Who are you going to bite first?" asked one of his brothers.

He answered very crossly: "I don't know and I don't care. I'm not hungry. Can't you think of anything but eating?"

"Why, what else is there to think about?" cried all the floating Mosquitoes.

"Well, there is flying," said he.

"Humph! I don't see what use flying would be except to carry us to our food," said one Mosquito Sister. She afterward found out that it was good for other reasons.

After that they didn't try to talk with their Oldest Brother. They talked with each other and tried their legs, and wished it were light enough for them to see their wings. Mosquitoes have such interesting wings, you know, thin and gauzy, and with delicate fringes around the edges and along the line of each vein. The sisters, too, were proud of the pockets under their wings, and were in a hurry to have their wings harden, so that they could flutter them and hear the beautiful singing sound made by the air striking these pockets. They knew that their brothers could never sing, and they were glad to think that they were ahead of them for once. It was not really their fault that they felt so, for the brothers had often put on airs and laughed at them.

Then came a wonderful flash of lightning and a long roll of thunder, and the trees tossed their beautiful branches to and fro, while big rain-drops pattered down on to the roof overhead and spattered and bounded and rolled toward the edge under which the rain-barrel stood.

"Fly!" cried the Oldest Brother, raising his wings as well as he could.

"We can't. Where to?" cried the rest.

"Fly any way, anywhere!" screamed the Oldest Brother, and in some wonderful way the whole twenty-three managed to flutter and crawl and sprawl up the side of the building, where the rain-drops fell past but did not touch them. There they found older Mosquitoes waiting for the shower to stop. Even the Oldest Brother was so scared that he shook, and when he was that same Mosquito Mother who had told him to put off changing his skin, he got behind two other young Mosquitoes and kept very still. Perhaps she saw him, for it was lighter then than it had been. She did not seem to see him, but he heard her talking to her friends. "I told him," she said, "that he might better put off moulting, but he answered that he could take care of himself, and that he would be out biting people before morning."

"Did he say that?" cried the other old Mosquitoes.

"He did," she replied.

Then they all laughed and laughed and laughed again, and the young Mosquito found out why. It was because Mosquito brothers have to eat honey, and only the sisters may bite people and suck their blood. He had thought so often how he would sing around somebody until he found the nicest, juiciest spot, and then settle lightly down and bite and suck until his slender little body was fat and round and red with its stomachful of blood. And that could never be! He could never sing, and he would have to sit around with his stomach full of honey and see his eleven sisters gorged with blood and hear them singing sweetly as they flew. If Mosquito Fathers had ever come to the barrel he might have found this out, but they never did. He sneaked off by himself until he met an early bird and then—well, you know birds must eat something, and the Mosquito was right there. Of course, after that, his brothers and sisters had a chance to do as they wanted to, and the eleven sisters bit thirteen people the very next night and had the loveliest kind of Mosquito time.

# THE NAUGHTY RACCOON
# CHILDREN

T HERE was hardly a night of his life when the Little Brother of the raccoon family was not reproved by his mother for teasing. Mrs. Raccoon said she didn't know what she had done to deserve such a child. When she spoke like this to her neighbors they sighed and said, "It must be trying, but he may outgrow it."

The Oldest Wolverene, though, told the Skunk that his cousin, Mrs. Raccoon's husband, had been just as bad as that when he was young. "I do not want you to say that I said so," he whispered, "because he might hear of it and be angry, but it is true." The Oldest Wolverene didn't say whether Mr. Raccoon outgrew this bad habit, yet it would seem that his wife had never noticed it.

You must not think that Mr. Raccoon was dead. Oh, no, indeed! Every night he was prowling through the forest on tiptoe looking for food. But Mrs. Raccoon was a very devoted mother and gave so much time and attention to her children that she was not good company for her husband. He did not

20

care much for home life, and the children annoyed him exceedingly, so he went away and found a hole in another tree which he fitted up for himself. There he slept through the day and until the setting of the sun told him that it was time for his breakfast. Raccoons like company, and he often had friends in to sleep with him. Sometimes these friends were Raccoons like himself with wives and children, and then they would talk about their families and tell how they thought their wives were spoiling the children.

The four little Raccoons, who lived with their mother in the dead branch of the big oak-tree, had been born in April, when the forest was sweet with the scent of wild violets and every one was happy. Beautiful pink and white trilliums raised their three-cornered flowers above their threefold leaves and nodded with every passing breeze. Yellow adder's-tongue was there, with cranesbill geraniums, squirrel-corn, and spring beauties, besides hepaticas and windflowers and the dainty bishop's-cap. The young Raccoons did not see these things, for their eyes would not work well by daylight, and when, after dark, their mother let them put their heads out of the hole and look around, they were too far from the ground to see the flowers sleeping in the dusk below. They could only sniff, sniff, sniff with their sharp little turned-up noses, and wonder what flowers look like, any way.

When their mother was with them for a time, and that was while they were drinking the warm milk that she always carried for them, she told them stories of the flowers and trees. She had begun by telling them animal stories, but she found that it made them cowardly. "Just supposing," one young Raccoon had said, "a great big, dreadful Snail should come up this tree and eat us all!"

The mother told them that Snails were small and slow and weak, and never climbed trees or ate people, but it did no good, and her children were always afraid of Snails until they had seen one for themselves. After that she told them stories of the flowers, and when they asked if the flowers would ever come to see them, she said, "No, indeed!" You will never see them until you can climb down the tree and walk among them, for they grow with their feet in the ground and never go anywhere." There were many stories which they wanted over and over again, but the one they liked best of all was that about the wicked, wicked Poison Ivy and the gentle Spotted Touch-me-not who grew near him and undid all the trouble that the Ivy made.

When the night came for the young Raccoons to climb down from their tree and learn to hunt, all the early spring blossoms were gone, and only the ripening seed-vessels showed where nodding flowers had been. You would have expected the Raccoon children to be disappointed, yet there were so many other things to see and learn about that it was not until three nights later that they thought much about the flowers. They might not have done so then if Little Sister had not lost her hold upon the oak-tree bark and fallen with her forepaws on a scarlet jack-in-the-pulpit berry.

They had to learn to climb quickly and strongly up all sorts of trees. Perhaps Mrs. Raccoon had chosen an oak for her nest because that was rough and easily climbed. There were many good places for Raccoons to grip with their twenty strong claws apiece. After they had learned oaks they took maples, ironwoods, and beeches—each a harder lesson than the one before.

"When you climb a tree," said their mother, "always look over the trunk and the largest branches for hiding-places, whether you want to use one then or not."

"Why?" asked three of the four children. Big Brother, who was rather vain, was looking at the five beautiful black rings and the beautiful black tip of his wonderful bushy tail. Between the black rings were whitish ones, and he thought such things much more interesting than holes in trees.

"Because," said the Mother Raccoon, "you may be far from home some night and want a safe place to sleep in all day. Or if a man and his Dogs are chasing you, you must climb into the first hiding-place you can. We Raccoons are too fat and slow to run away from them, and the rings on our tails and the black patches on our broad faces might show from the ground. If the hole is a small one, make it cover your head and your tail anyway, and as much of your brown body fur as you can."

Mother Raccoon looked sternly at Big Brother because he had not been listening, and he gave a slight jump and asked, "W-what did you say?"

"What did I say?" she replied. "You should have paid better attention."

"Yes'm," said Big Brother, who was now very meek.

"I shall not repeat it," said his mother, "but I will tell you not to grow vain of your fur. It is very handsome, and so is that of your sisters and your brother. So is mine, and so was your father's the last time I saw him. Yet nearly all the trouble that Raccoons have is on account of their fur. Never try to show it off."

The time came for the young Raccoons to stop drinking milk from their mother's body, and when they tried to do so she only walked away from them.

"I cannot work so hard to care for you," said she. "I am so tired and thin, now, that my skin is loose, and you must find your own food. You are getting forty fine teeth apiece, and I never saw a better lot of claws on any Raccoon family, if I do say it."

They used to go hunting together, for it is the custom for Raccoons to go in parties of from five to eight, hunt all night, and then hide somewhere until the next night. They did not always come home at sunrise, and it made a pleasant change to sleep in different trees. One day they all cuddled down in the hollow of an old maple, just below where the branches come out. Mother Raccoon had climbed the tree first and was curled away in the very bottom of the hole. The four children were not tired and hadn't wanted to go to bed at all. Little Sister had made a dreadful face when her mother called her up the tree, and if it had not already been growing light, Mrs. Raccoon would probably have seen it and punished her.

Big Sister curled down beside her mother and Little Sister was rather above them and beside mischievous Little Brother. Last of all came Big Brother, who had stopped to scratch his ear with his hind foot. He was very proud of his little round ears, and often scratched them in this way to make sure that the fur lay straight on them. He was so slow in reaching the hole that before he got into it a Robin had begun his morning song of "Cheerily, cheerily, cheer-up!" and a Chipmunk perched on a stump to make his morning toilet.

He got all settled, and Little Brother was half asleep beside him, when he remembered his tail and sat up to have one more look at it. Little Brother growled sleepily and told him to "let his old tail alone and come to bed, as long as they couldn't hunt any more." But Big Brother thought he saw a sand-burr on his tail, and wanted to pull it out before it hurt the fur. Then he began to look at the bare, tough pads on his feet, and to notice how finely he could spread his toes. Those of his front feet he could spread especially wide. He balanced himself on the edge of the hole and held them spread out before him. It was still dark enough for him to see well. "Come here, Little Brother," he cried. "Wake up, and see how big my feet are getting."

Mother Raccoon growled at them to be good children and go to sleep, but her voice sounded dreamy and far away because she had to talk through part of her own fur and most of her daughters'.

Little Brother lost his patience, unrolled himself with a spring, jumped to the opening, and knocked his brother down. It was dreadful. Of course Big Brother was not much hurt, for he was very fat and his fur was both long and thick, but he turned over and over on his way to the ground before he alighted on his feet. He turned so fast and Little Brother's eyes hurt him so that it looked as though Big Brother had about three heads, three tails, and twelve feet. He called out as he fell, and that awakened the sisters, who began to cry, and Mother Raccoon, who was so scared that she began to scold.

Such a time! Mother Raccoon found out what had happened, and then she said, to Little Brother, "Did you mean to push him down?"

"No, ma'am," answered Little Brother, hanging his head. "Anyhow I didn't mean to after I saw him going. Perhaps I did mean to before that." You see he was a truthful Raccoon even when he was most naughty, and there is always hope for a Raccoon who will tell the truth, no matter how hard it is to do so.

Big Brother climbed slowly up the trunk of the oak-tree, while more and more of the daytime people came to look at him. He could not see well now, and so was very awkward. When he reached

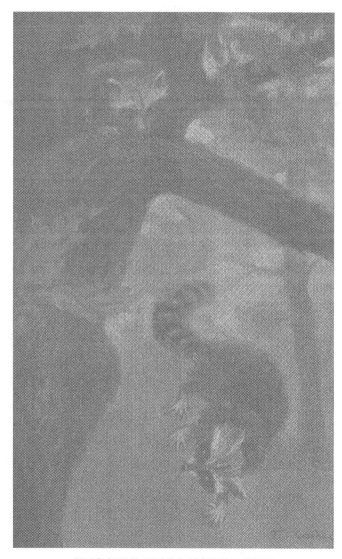

KNOCKED HIS BROTHER DOWN.

the hole he was hot and cross, and complained to his mother. "Make him quit teasing me," he said, pointing one forepaw at Little Brother.

"I will," answered Mother Raccoon; "but you were just as much to blame as he, for if you had cuddled down quietly when I told you to, you would have been dreaming long ago. Now you must sleep where I was, at the lower end of the hole. Little Brother must go next, and I do not want to hear one word from either of you. Sisters next, and I will sleep by the opening. You children must remember that it is no time for talking to each other, or looking at claws, or getting sand-burrs out of your tails after you have been sent to bed. Go to sleep, and don't awaken until the sun has gone down and you are ready to be my good little Raccoons again."

Her children were asleep long before she was, and she talked softly to herself after they were dreaming. "They do not mean to be naughty," she said. "Yet it makes my fur stand on end to think what might have happened. . . . I ought not to have curled up for the day until they had done so. . . . Mothers should always be at the top of the heap." Then she fixed herself for a long, restful day's sleep.

# THE TIMID LITTLE GROUND
# HOG

IT was not often that the little Ground Hogs were left alone in the daytime. Before they were born their mother had been heard to say that she had her opinion of any Ground Hog who would be seen out after sunrise. Mr. Ground Hog felt in the same way, and said if he ever got to running around by daylight, like some of his relatives, people might call him a Woodchuck. He thought that any one who ate twigs, beets, turnips, young tree-bark, and other green things from sunset to sunrise ought to be able to get along until the next sunset without a lunch. He said that any Ground Hog who wanted more was a Pig.

After the baby Ground Hogs were born, matters were different. They could not go out at night to feed for themselves, and their stomachs were so tiny and held so little at a time that they had to be filled very often. Mr. Ground Hog was never at home now, and the care all fell upon his hard-working wife.

"You know, my dear," he had said, "that I should only be in the way if I were to stay at home, for I am not clever and patient with children as you are. No, I think I will go away and see to some matters which I have rather neglected of late. When the children are grown up and you have more time to give me, I will come back to you."

Then Mr. Ground Hog trotted away to join a party of his friends who had just told their wives something of the same sort, and they all went together to the farmer's turnip patch and had a delightful time until morning. Mrs. Ground Hog looked after him as he trotted away and wished that she could go too. He looked so handsome with the moonlight shining down on his long, thick, reddish fur, and showing the black streak on his back where the fur was tipped with gray. He was fat and shaky, with a baggy skin, and when he stopped to sit up on his haunches and wave his paws at her and comb his face-fur, she thought him just as handsome as he had been in the early spring when they first met. That had been in a parsnip patch where there was good feeding until the farmer found that the Ground Hogs were there, and dug the rest of his vegetables and stored them in his cellar. Such midnight meals as they had eaten there together! Mrs. Ground Hog said she never saw a parsnip afterward without thinking of their courtship.

She had been as handsome as he, and there were many other Ground Hogs who admired her. But now she was thin and did not have many chances to comb her fur with her fore paws. She could not go with him to the turnip patch because she did not wish to go so far from her babies. Thinking of that reminded her to go into her sidehill burrow and see what they were doing. Then she lay down and let them draw the warm milk from her body. While they were feeding she felt of them, and thought how fast they were growing. It would be only a short time before they could trot around the fields by themselves and whistle shrilly as they dodged down into their own burrows. "Ah!" said she, "this is better than turnip patches or even parsnips."

When they had finished, their mother left them and went out to feed. She had always been a hearty eater, but now she had to eat enough more to make the milk for her babies. She often thought that if Ground Hog babies could eat anything else their father might have learned to help feed them. She thought of this especially when she saw the Great Horned Owl carrying food home to his son and daughter. "It is what comes of being four-legged," said she, "and I wouldn't be an Owl for anything, so I won't grumble." After this she was more cheerful.

When she left the burrow she always said: "I am going out to feed, and I shall not be gone very long. Don't be afraid, for you have a good burrow, and it is nice and dark outside."

The children would cry: "And you will surely come home before sunrise?"

"Surely," she always answered as she trotted away. Then the children would rest happily in their burrow-nest.

But now Mrs. Ground Hog was hungry, and it was broad daylight. She knew that it was because her children grew bigger every day and had to have more and more milk. This meant that she must eat more, or else when they wanted milk there would not be enough ready. She knew that she must begin to feed by day as well as by night, and she was glad that she could see fairly well if the sun were not shining into her eyes.

"Children," said she to them, just as they finished their morning lunch, "I am very hungry and I am going out to feed. You will be quite safe here and I want you to be good while I am gone."

The young Ground Hogs began to cry and clutch at her fur with their weak little paws. "Oh, don't go," they said. "Please don't go. We don't want to stay alone in the daytime. We're afraid."

"I must," said she, "or I shall have no milk for you. And then, you wouldn't have me lie here all day too hungry to sleep, would you?"

"N-no," said they; "but you'll come back soon, won't you?"

"Yes," said she, and she shook off their clinging paws and poked back the daughter who caught on again, and trotted away as fast as she could. It was the first time that she had been out by daylight, and everything looked queer. The colors looked too bright, and there seemed to be more noise than usual, and she met several people whom she had never seen before. She stopped for a minute to look at an Ovenbird's nest. The mother-bird was inside, sitting there very still and brave, although she was much frightened.

"Good-morning," said Mrs. Ground Hog. "I was just admiring your nest. I have never seen it by daylight."

"Good-morning," answered the Ovenbird. "I'm glad you fancy my nest, but I hope you don't like to eat meat."

"Meat?" answered Mrs. Ground Hog. "I never touch it." And she smiled and showed all her teeth.

"Oh," exclaimed the Ovenbird, "I see you don't, for you have gnawing-teeth, rather like those of the Rabbits." Then she hopped out of the nest and let Mrs. Ground Hog peep in to see how the inside was finished and also to see the four speckled eggs which lay there.

"It is a lovely nest," said Mrs. Ground Hog, "and those eggs are beauties. But I promised the children that I would hurry. Good-by." She trotted happily away, while Mrs. Ovenbird settled herself upon her eggs again and thought what a pleasant call she had had and what an excellent and intelligent person Mrs. Ground Hog was!

All this time the children at home were talking together about themselves and what their mother had told them. Once there was a long pause which lasted until the brother said: "I'm not afraid, are you?"

"Of course not," said they.

"Because there isn't anything to be afraid of," said he.

"Not anything," said they.

"And I wouldn't be afraid anyway," said he.

"Neither would we," answered the sisters.

There was another long pause.

"She said we'd be just as safe as if it were dark," said the big sister.

"Of course," said the brother.

"And she said she'd come back as soon as she could," said the second sister.

"I wish she'd come now," said the smallest sister.

There was another long pause.

"You don't suppose anybody would come here just to scare us, do you?" asked the second sister.

"See here," said the brother, "I wish you'd quit saying things to make a fellow afraid."

"You don't mean that you are frightened!" exclaimed the three sisters together. And the smallest one added: "Why, you are, too! I can feel you tremble."

"Well, I don't care," said the brother. "I'm not afraid of people, anyhow. If it were only dark I wouldn't mind."

"Oh, are you afraid of the daylight too?" cried each of the sisters. "So am I!" Then they all trembled together.

"I tell you what let's do," said the smallest sister. "Let's all stop looking toward the light end of the burrow, and cuddle up together and cover our eyes and make believe it's night." They did this and felt better. They even played that they heard the few noises of the night-time. A Crow cawed outside, and the brother said, "Did you hear that Owl? That was the Great Horned Owl, the one who had to hatch the eggs, you know."

When another Crow cawed, the smallest sister said, "Was that his cousin, the Screech Owl?"

"Yes," answered the big sister. "He is the one who used to bring things for the Great Horned Owl to eat."

So they amused themselves and each other, and really got along very well except when, once in a while, they opened their eyes a little crack to see if it were not getting really dark. Then they had to begin all over again. At last their mother came, and what a comfort it was! How glad she was to be back, and how much she had to tell them! All about the Ovenbird's nest and the four eggs in it, and how the Ovenbirds spent their nights in sleeping and their days in work and play.

"I wonder if the little Ovenbirds will be scared when they have to stay alone in the daytime?" said the smallest sister.

"They would be more scared if they had to stay alone at night," said their mother.

"At night!" exclaimed all the young Ground Hogs. "Why, it is dark then!"

"They might be afraid of the darkness," said their mother. Then the children laughed and thought she was making fun of them. They drank some milk and went to sleep like good little Ground Hogs, but even after he was half asleep the big brother laughed out loud at the thought of the Ovenbird babies being scared at night. He could understand any one's being afraid of daylight, but darkness——!

# THE YOUNG RACCOONS GO
# TO A PARTY

IT was not very many nights after Big Brother had tumbled from the maple-tree, when he and the other children were invited to a Raccoon party down by the pond. The water was low, and in the small pools by the shore there were many fresh-water clams and small fishes, such as Raccoons like best of all. A family of six young Raccoons who lived very near the pond had found them just before sunrise, when they had to climb off to bed. They knew there was much more food there than they could eat alone, so their mother had let them invite their four friends who lived in the hollow of the oak-tree. The party was to begin the next evening at moonrise, and the four children who lived in the oak-tree got their invitation just as they were going to sleep for the day. They were very much excited over it, for they had never been to a party.

"I wish we could go now," said Big Brother.

"Yes, lots of fun it would be now!" answered Little Brother. "The sun is almost up, and there are no clouds in the sky. We couldn't see a thing unless we shaded our eyes with our fore paws, and if we had to use our fore paws in that way we couldn't eat."

"You do eat at parties, don't you?" asked Little Sister, who had not quite understood what was said.

"Of course," shouted her brothers. "That is what parties are for."

"I thought maybe you talked some," said Big Sister.

"I suppose you do have to, some," said Big Brother, "but I know you eat. I've heard people tell about parties lots of times, and they always began by telling what they ate. That's what makes it a party."

"Oh, I wish it were night and time to go," sighed Little Brother.

"I don't," said Little Sister. "I wouldn't have any fun if I were to go now. I'd rather wait until my stomach is empty."

"There!" said their mother. "You children have talked long enough. Now curl down and go to sleep. The birds are already singing their morning songs, and the Owls and Bats were dreaming long ago. It will make night-time come much sooner if you do not stay awake."

"We're not a big sleepy," cried all the young Raccoons together.

"That makes no difference at all," said their mother, and she spoke quite sternly. "Cuddle down for the day now, cover your eyes, and stop talking. I do not say you must sleep, but you must stop talking."

They knew that when she spoke in that way and said "must," there was nothing to do but to mind. So they cuddled down, and every one of them was asleep before you could drop an acorn. Mother Raccoon had known it would be so.

When they awakened, early the next night, each young Raccoon had to make himself look as neat as possible. There were long fur to be combed, faces and paws to be washed, and twenty-three burrs to be taken out of Little Brother's tail. He began to take them out himself, but his mother found that whenever he got one loose he stuck it onto one of the other children, so she scolded him and made him sit on a branch by himself while she worked at the burrs. Sometimes she couldn't help pulling the fur, and then he tried to wriggle away.

"You've got enough out," he cried. "Let the rest go."

"You should have thought sooner how it would hurt," she said. "You have been told again and again to keep away from the burrs, and you are just as careless as you were the first night you left the tree." Then she took out another burr and dropped it to the ground.

"Ouch!" said he. "Let me go!"

"Not until I am done," she answered. "No child of mine shall ever go to a party looking as you do."

After that Little Brother tried to hold still, and he had time to think how glad he was that he hadn't stuck any more burrs on the other children. If he had gotten more onto them, he would have had to wait while they were pulled off again, and then they might have been late for the party. If he had been very good, he would have been glad they didn't have to be hurt as he was. But he was not very good, and he never thought of that.

When he was ready at last, Mother Raccoon made her four children sit in a row while she talked to them. "Remember to walk on your toes," said she, "although you may stand flat-footed if you wish. Don't act greedy if you can help it. Go into the water as much as you choose, but don't try to dive, even if they dare you to. Raccoons can never learn to dive, no matter how well they swim. And be sure to wash your food before you eat it."

All the young Raccoons said, "Yes'm," and thought they would remember every word. The first moonbeam shone on the top of the oak-tree, and Mrs. Raccoon said: "Now you may go. Be good children and remember what I told you. Don't stay too long. Start home when you see the first light in the east."

"Yes'm," said the young Raccoons, as they walked off very properly toward the pond. After they were well away from the oak-tree, they heard their mother calling to them: "Remember to walk on your toes!"

Raccoons cannot go very fast, and the moon was shining brightly when they reached the pond and met their six friends. Such frolics as they had in the shallow water, swimming, twisting, turning, scooping up food with their busy fore paws, going up and down the beach, and rolling on the sand! They never once remembered what their mother had told them, and they acted exactly as they had been in the habit of doing every day. Big Brother looked admiringly at his own tail every chance he got, although he had been told particularly not to act as if he thought himself fine-looking. Little Brother rolled into a lot of sandburs and got his fur so matted that he looked worse than ever. Big Sister snatched food from other Raccoons, and not one of them remembered about walking on tiptoe. Little Sister ate half the time without washing her food. Of course that didn't matter when the food was taken from the pond, but when they found some on the beach and ate it without washing—that was dreadful. No Raccoon who is anybody at all will do that.

The mother of the family of six looked on from a tree near by. The children did not know that she was there. "What manners!" said she. "I shall never have them invited here again." Just then she saw one of her own sons eat without washing his food, and she groaned out loud. "My children are forgetting too," she said. "I have told him hundreds of times that if he did that way every day he would

41

do so at a party, but he has always said he would remember."

The mother of the four young Raccoons was out hunting and found herself near the pond. "How noisy those children are!" she said to herself. "Night people should be quiet." She tiptoed along to a pile of rocks and peeped between them to see what was going on. She saw her children's footprints on the sand. "Aha!" said she. "So they did walk flat-footed after all."

She heard somebody scrambling down a tree nearby. "Good-evening," said a pleasant Raccoon voice near her. It was the mother of the six. "Are you watching the children's party?" asked the newcomer. "I hope you did not notice how badly my son is behaving. I have tried to teach my children good manners, but they will be careless when I am not looking, and then, of course, they forget in company."

That made the mother of the four feel more comfortable. "I know just how that is," said she. "Mine mean to be good, but they are so careless. It is very discouraging."

The two mothers talked for a long time in whispers and then each went to her hole.

When the four young Raccoons came home, it was beginning to grow light, and they kept close together because they were somewhat afraid. Their mother was waiting to see them settled for the day. She asked if they had a good time, and said she was glad they got home promptly. They had been afraid she would ask if they had washed their food and walked on their toes. She even seemed not to notice Little Brother's matted coat.

When they awakened the next night, the mother hurried them off with her to the same pond where they had been to the party. "I am going to visit with the mother of your friends," said she, "and you may play around and amuse yourselves."

The young Raccoons had another fine time, although Little Brother found it very uncomfortable to wear so many burrs. They played tag in the trees, and ate, and swam, and lay on the beach. While they were lying there, the four from the oak-tree noticed that their mother was walking flat-footed. There was bright moonlight and anybody might see her. They felt dreadfully about it. Then they saw her begin to eat food which she had not washed. They were so ashamed that they didn't want to look their friends in the eye. They didn't know that their friends were feeling in the same way because they had seen their mother doing ill-mannered things.

After they reached home, Big Brother said, very timidly, to his mother: "Did you know you ate some food without washing it?"

"Oh, yes," she answered; "it is such a bother to dip it all in water."

"And you walked flat-footed," said Little Brother.

"Well, why shouldn't I, if I want to?" said she.

43

The children began to cry: "P-people will think you don't know any b-better," said they. "We were d-dreadfully ashamed."

"Oh!" said their mother. "Oh! Oh! So you think that my manners are not so good as yours! Is that it?"

The young Raccoons looked at each other in a very uncomfortable way. "We suppose we don't always do things right ourselves," they answered, "but you are grown up."

"Yes," replied their mother. "And you will be."

For a long time nobody spoke, and Little Sister sobbed out loud. Then Mrs. Raccoon spoke more gently: "The sun is rising," said she. "We will go to sleep now, and when we awaken to-morrow night we will try to have better manners, so that we need not be ashamed of each other at parties or at home."

Long after the rest were dreaming, Big Sister nudged Big Brother and awakened him. "I understand it now," she said. "She did it on purpose."

"Who did what?" asked he.

"Why, our mother. She was rude on purpose to let us see how it looked."

Big Brother thought for a minute. "Of course," said he. "Of course she did! Well she won't ever have to do it again for me."

"Nor for me," said Big Sister. Then they went to sleep.

# THE SKUNKS AND THE OVENBIRD'S NEST

THE Skunks did not go into society at all. They were very unpopular, and so many people feared or disliked them that nobody would invite them to a party. Indeed, if they had been invited to a party and had gone, the other guests would have left at once. The small people of the forest feared them because they were meat-eaters, and the larger ones disliked them because of their disagreeable habits. The Skunks were handsome and quiet, but they were quick-tempered, and as soon as one of them became angry he threw a horrible smelling liquid on the people who displeased him. It was not only horrible smelling, but it made those who had to smell it steadily quite sick, and would, indeed, have killed them if they had not kept in the fresh air. If a drop of this liquid got on to a person, even his wife and children had to keep away from him for a long time.

And the Skunks were so unreasonable. They would not stop to see what was the real trouble, but if anybody ran into them by mistake in the darkness, they would just as likely as not throw the liquid at once. Among themselves they seemed to be quite happy. There were from six to ten children born at a time in each family. These children lived in the burrow with their father and mother until the next spring, sleeping steadily through the coldest weather of winter, and only awakening when it was warm enough for them to enjoy life. When spring came, the children found themselves grown-up and went off to live their own lives in new holes, while their mothers took care of the six or seven or eight or nine or ten new babies.

There was one very interesting Skunk family in the forest, with the father, mother, and eight children living in one hole. No two of them were marked in exactly the same way, although all were stoutly built, had small heads, little round ears, and beautiful long tails covered with soft, drooping hair. Their fur was rather long and handsome and they were dark brown or black nearly all over. Most of them had a streak of white on the forehead, a spot of it on the neck, some on the tail, and a couple of stripes of it on their backs. One could see them quite easily by starlight on account of the white fur.

The Skunks were really proud of their white stripes and spots. "It is not so much having the white fur," Mrs. Skunk had been heard to say, "as it is having it where all can see it. Most animals wear the dark fur on their backs and the light on their bellies, and that is to make them safer from enemies. But we dare to wear ours in plain sight. *We* are never afraid."

And what she said was true, although it hardly seemed modest for her to talk about it in that way. It would have been more polite to let other people tell how brave her family were. Perhaps, however, if somebody else had been telling it, he would have said that part of their courage was rudeness.

Father Skunk always talked to his children as his father had talked to him, and probably as his grandfather had also talked when he was raising a family. "Never turn out of your way for anybody," said he. "Let the other fellow step aside. Remember that, no matter whom you meet and no matter how large the other people may be. If they see you, they will get out of your path, and if they can't it is not your fault. Don't speak to them and don't hurry. Always take your time."

Father Skunk was slow and stately. It was a sight worth seeing when he started off for a night's ramble, walking with a slow and measured gait and carrying his fine tail high over his back. He always went by himself. "One is company, two is a crowd," he would say as he walked away. When they were old enough, the young Skunks began to walk off alone as soon as it was dark. Mother Skunk also went alone, and perhaps she had the best time of all, for it was a great rest not to have eight babies tumbling over her back and getting under her feet and hanging on to her with their thirty-two paws, and sometimes even scratching her with their one hundred and sixty claws. They still slept through the days in the old hole, so they were together much of the time, but

HE STARTED OFF FOR A NIGHT'S RAMBLE.

they did not hunt in parties, as Raccoons and Weasels do.

One of the brothers had no white whatever on his tail, so they called him the Black-tailed Skunk. He had heard in some way that there was an Ovenbird's nest on the ground by the fern bank, and he made up his mind to find it the very next night and eat the eggs which were inside.

Another brother was called the Spotted Skunk, because the spot on his neck was so large. He had found the Ovenbird's nest himself, while on his way home in the early morning. He would have liked to rob it then, but he had eaten so much that night that he thought it better to wait.

So it happened that when the family awakened the next night two of the children had important plans of their own. Neither of them would have told for anything, but they couldn't quite keep from hinting about it as they made themselves ready to go out.

"Aha!" said the Black-tailed Skunk. "I know something you don't know."

"Oh, tell us!" cried four or five of the other children, while the Spotted Skunk twisted his head and said, "You don't either!"

"I do too!" replied the Black-tailed Skunk.

"Children! Children!" exclaimed Mrs. Skunk, while their father said that he couldn't see where his children got their quarrelsome disposition, for none of his people had ever contradicted or disputed. His wife told him that she really thought them very good, and that she was sure they behaved much better than most Skunks of their age. Then their father walked off in his most stately manner, putting his feet down almost flat, and carrying his tail a little higher than usual.

"I do know something that you don't," repeated the Black-tailed Skunk, "and it's something nice, too."

"Aw!" said the Spotted Skunk. "I don't believe it, and I don't care anyhow."

"I know you don't know, and I know you'd want to know if you knew what I know," said the Black-tailed Skunk, who was now getting so excited that he could hardly talk straight.

"Children!" exclaimed their mother. "Not another word about that. I do wish you would wake up good-natured."

"He started it," said the Spotted Skunk, "and we're not quarrelling anyhow. But I guess he'd give a good deal to know where I'm going."

"Children!" repeated their mother. "Go at once. I will not have you talking in this way before your brothers and sisters. Do not stop to talk, but go!"

So the two brothers started out for the night and each thought he would go a roundabout way to fool the other. The Black-tailed Skunk went to the right, and the Spotted Skunk went to the left, but each of them, you know, really started to rob the

Ovenbird's nest. It was a very dark night. Even the stars were all hidden behind thick clouds, and one could hardly see one's forepaws while walking. But, of course, the night-prowlers of the forest are used to this, and four-footed people are not so likely to stumble and fall as two-footed ones. Besides, young Skunks have to remember where logs and stumps of trees are, just as other people have to remember their lessons.

So it happened that, while Mrs. Ovenbird was sleeping happily with her four eggs safe and warm under her breast, two people were coming from different ways to rob her. Such a snug nest as it was! She had chosen a tiny hollow in the fern bank and had cunningly woven dry grasses and leaves into a ball-shaped nest, which fitted neatly into the hollow and had a doorway on one side.

The Black-tailed Skunk sneaked up to the nest from one side. The Spotted Skunk sneaked up from the other side. Once the Black-tailed Skunk thought he heard some other creature moving toward him. At the same minute the Spotted Skunk thought he heard somebody, so he stopped to listen. Neither heard anything. Mrs. Ovenbird was sure that she heard a leaf rustle outside, and it made her anxious until she remembered that a dead twig might have dropped from the beech-tree overhead and hit the dry leaves below.

Slowly the two brothers crept toward the nest and each other. They moved very quietly, because each wanted to catch the mother-bird if he could.

Close to the nest hollow they crouched and sprang with jaws open and sharp teeth ready to bite. There was a sudden crashing of leaves and ferns. The two brothers had sprung squarely at each other, each was bitten, growled, and ran away. And how they did run! It is not often, you know, that Skunks go faster than a walk, but when they are really scared they move very, very swiftly.

Mrs. Ovenbird felt her nest roof crush down upon her for a minute as two people rolled and growled outside. Then she heard them running away in different directions and knew that she was safe, for a time at least. In the morning she repaired her nest and told her bird friends about it. They advised her to take her children away as soon as possible after they were hatched. "If the Skunks have found your nest," they said, "you may have another call from them."

When the Black-tailed Skunk came stealing home in the first faint light just before sunrise, he found the Spotted Skunk telling the rest of the family how some horrible great fierce beast had pounced upon him in the darkness and bitten him on the shoulder. "It was so dark," said he, "that I couldn't see him at all, but I am sure it must have been a Bear."

They turned to tell the Black-tailed Skunk about his brother's misfortune, and saw that he limped badly. "Did the Bear catch you, too?" they cried.

"Yes," answered he. "It must have been a Bear. It was so big and strong and fierce. But I bit him, too. I wouldn't have run away from him, only he was so much bigger than I."

"That was just the way with me," said the Spotted Skunk. "I wouldn't have run if he hadn't been so big."

"You should have thrown liquid on him," said their father. "Then he would have been the one to run."

"The brothers hung their heads. "We never thought," they cried. "We think it must have been because we were so surprised and didn't see him coming."

"Well," said their father sternly, "I suppose one must be patient with children, but such unskunklike behavior makes me very much ashamed of you both." Then the two bitten brothers went to bed in disgrace, although their mother was sorry for them and loved them, as mothers will do, even when their children are naughty or cowardly.

One night, some time later, these two brothers happened to meet down by the fern bank. It was bright moonlight and they stopped to visit, for both were feeling very good-natured. The Black-tailed Skunk said: "Come with me and I'll show you where there is an Ovenbird's nest."

"All right," answered the Spotted Skunk, "and then I'll show you one."

"I've just been waiting for a bright night," said the Black-tailed Skunk, "because I came here once in the dark and had bad luck."

"It was near here," said the Spotted Skunk, "that I was bitten by the Bear."

They stopped beside a tiny hollow. "There is the nest," said the Black-tailed Skunk, pointing with one of his long forefeet.

"Why that is the one I meant," exclaimed the Spotted Skunk.

"I found it first," said the Black-tailed Skunk, "and I'd have eaten the eggs before if that Bear hadn't bitten me."

Just at that minute the two Skunks had a new idea. "We do believe," cried they, "that we bit each other!"

"We certainly did," said the Spotted Skunk.

"But we'll never tell," said the Black-tailed Skunk.

"Now," they added together, "let's eat everything."

But they didn't. In fact, they didn't eat anything, for the eggs were hatched, and the young birds had left the nest only the day before.

# THE LAZY CUT-WORMS

NOW that spring had come and all the green things were growing, the Cut-Worms crawled out of their winter sleeping-places in the ground, and began to eat the tenderest and best things that they could find. They felt rested and hungry after their quiet winter, for they had slept without awakening ever since the first really cold days of fall.

There were many different kinds of Cut-Worms, brothers and sisters, cousins and second cousins, so, of course, they did not all look alike. They had hatched the summer before from eggs laid by the Owlet Moths, their mothers, and had spent the time from then until cold weather in eating and sleeping and eating some more. Of course they grew a great deal, but then, you know, one can grow without taking time especially for it. It is well that this is so. If people had to say, "I can do nothing else now. I must sit down and grow awhile," there would not be so many large people in the world as there are. They would become so interested in doing other things that they would not take the time to grow as they should.

Now the Cut-Worms were fine and fat and just as heedless as Cut-Worms have been since the world began. They had never seen their parents, and had hatched without any one to look after them. They did not look like their parents, for they were only worms as yet, but they had the same habit of sleeping all day and going out at night, and never thought of eating breakfast until the sun had gone down. They were quite popular in underground society, and were much liked by the Earthworms and May Beetle larvæ, who enjoyed hearing stories of what the Cut-Worms saw above ground. The May Beetle larvæ did not go out at all, because they were too young, and the Earthworms never knew what was going on outside unless somebody told them. They often put their heads up into the air, but they had no eyes and could not see for themselves.

The Cut-Worms were bold, saucy, selfish, and wasteful. They were not good children, although when they tried they could be very entertaining, and one always hoped that they would improve before they became Moths. Sometimes they even told the Earthworms and May Beetle larvæ stories that were not so, and that shows what sort of children they were. It was dreadful to tell such things to people who could never find out the difference. One Spotted Cut-Worm heard a couple of Earthworms talking about Ground Moles, and told them that Ground Moles were large birds with four wings apiece and legs like a Caterpillar's. They did not take pains to be entertaining because they wanted to make the underground people happy, but because they enjoyed hearing them say: "What bright fellows those Cut-Worms are! Really exceedingly clever!" And doing it for that reason took all the goodness out of it.

One bright moonlight night the Cut-Worms awakened and crawled out on top of the ground to feed. They lived in the farmer's vegetable garden, so there were many things to choose from: young beets just showing their red-veined leaves above their shining red stems; turnips; clean-looking onions holding their slender leaves very stiff and straight; radishes with just a bit of their rosy roots peeping out of the earth; and crisp, pale green lettuce, crinkled and shaking in every passing breeze. It was a lovely growing time, and all the vegetables were making the most of the fine nights, for, you know, that is the time when everything grows best. Sunshiny days are the best for coloring leaves and blossoms, but the time for sinking roots deeper and sending shoots higher and unfolding new leaves is at night in the beautiful stillness.

Some Cut-Worms chose beets and some chose radishes. Two or three liked lettuce best, and a couple crawled off to nibble at the sweet peas which the farmer's wife had planted. They never ate all of a plant. Ah, no! And that was one way in which they were wasteful. They nibbled through the stalk where it came out of the ground, and then the plant tumbled down and withered, while the Cut-Worm went on to treat another in the same way.

"Well!" exclaimed one Spotted Cut-Worm, as he crawled out from his hole. "I must have overslept! Guess I stayed up too late this morning."

"You'd better look out," said one of his friends, "or the Ground Mole will get you. He likes to find nice fat little Cut-Worms who sleep too late in the evening."

"Needn't tell me," answered the Spotted Cut-Worm. "It's the early Mole that catches the Cut-Worm. I don't know when I have overslept myself so. Have you fellows been up ever since sunset?"

"Yes," they answered; and one saucy fellow added: "I got up too early. I awakened and felt hungry, and thought I'd just come out for a lunch. I supposed the birds had finished their supper, but the first thing I saw was a Robin out hunting. She was not more than the length of a bean-pole from me, and when I saw her cock her head on one side and look toward me, I was sure she saw me. But she didn't, after all. Lucky for me that I am green and came up beside the lettuce. I kept still and she took me for a leaf."

"St!" said somebody else. "There comes the Ground Mole." They all kept still while the Mole scampered to and fro on the dewy grass near them, going faster than one would think he could with such very, very short legs. His pink digging hands flashed in the moonlight, and his pink snout showed also, but the dark, soft fur of the rest of his body could hardly be seen against the brown earth of the garden. It may have been because he was not hungry, or it may have been because his fur covered over his eyes so, but he went back to his underground run-way without having caught a single Cut-Worm.

Then the Cut-Worms felt very much set up. They crawled toward the hole into his run-way and made faces at it, as though he were standing in the doorway. They called mean things after him and pretended to say them very loudly, yet really spoke quite softly.

Then they began to boast that they were not afraid of anybody, and while they were boasting they ate and ate and ate and ate. Here and there the young plants drooped and fell over, and as soon as one did that, the Cut-Worm who had eaten on it crawled off to another.

"Guess the farmer will know that we've been here," said they. "We don't care. He doesn't need all these vegetables. What if he did plant them? Let him plant some more if he wants to. What business has he to have so many, anyhow, if he won't share with other people?" You would have thought, to hear them, that they were exceedingly kind to leave any vegetables for the farmer.

In among the sweet peas were many little tufts of purslane, and purslane is very good to eat, as anybody knows who has tried it. But do you think the Cut-Worms ate that? Not a bit of it. "We can have purslane any day," they said, "and now we will eat sweet peas."

One little fellow added: "You won't catch me eating purslane. It's a weed." Now, Cut-Worms do eat weeds, but they always seem to like best those things which have been carefully planted and tended. If the purslane had been set in straight rows, and the sweet peas had just come up of themselves everywhere, it is quite likely that this young Cut-Worm would have said: "You won't catch me eating sweet peas. They are weeds."

As the moon rose higher and higher in the sky, the Cut-Worms boasted more and more. They said there were no Robins clever enough to find them, and that the Ground Mole dared not touch them when they were together, and that it was only when he found one alone underground that he was brave enough to do so. They talked very loudly now and bragged dreadfully, until they noticed that the moon was setting and a faint yellow light showed over the tree-tops in the east.

"Time to go to bed for the day," called the Spotted Cut-Worm. "Where are you going to crawl in?" They had no regular homes, you know, but crawled into the earth wherever they wanted to and slept until the next night.

"Here are some fine holes already made," said a Green Cut-Worm, "and big enough for a Garter Snake. They are smooth and deep, and a lot of us can cuddle down into each. I'm going into one of them."

"Who made those holes?" asked the Spotted Cut-Worm; "and why are they here?"

"Oh, who cares who made them?" answered the Green Cut-Worm. "Guess they're ours if we want to use them."

"Perhaps the farmer made them," said the Spotted Cut-Worm, "and if he did I don't want to go into them."

"Oh, who's afraid of him?" cried the other Cut-Worms. "Come along!"

"No," answered the Spotted Cut-Worm. "I won't. I don't want to and I won't do it. The hole I make to sleep in will not be so large, nor will it have such smooth sides, but I'll know all about it and feel safe. Good morning!" Then he crawled into the earth and went to sleep. The others went into the smooth, deep holes made by the farmer with his hoe handle.

The next night there was only one Cut-Worm in the garden, and that was the Spotted Cut-Worm. Nobody has ever seen the lazy ones who chose to use the smooth, deep holes which were ready made. The Spotted Cut-Worm lived quite alone until he was full-grown, then he made a little oval room for himself in the ground and slept in it while he changed into a Black Owlet Moth.

After that he flew away to find a wife and live among her people. It is said that whenever he saw a Cut-Worm working at night, he would flutter down beside him and whisper,—"The Cut-Worm who is too lazy to bore his own sleeping-place will never live to become an Owlet Moth."

# THE NIGHT MOTH'S PARTY

FROM the time when she was a tiny golden-green Caterpillar, Miss Polyphemus had wanted to go into society. She began life on a maple leaf with a few brothers and sisters, who hatched at the same time from a cluster of flattened eggs which their mother had laid there ten days before. The first thing she remembered was the light and color and sound when she broke the shell open that May morning. The first thing she did was to eat the shell out of which she had just crawled. Then she got acquainted with her brothers and sisters, many of whom had also eaten their eggshells, although two had begun at once on maple leaves. It was well that she took time for this now, for the family were soon scattered and several of her sisters she never saw again.

She found it a very lovely world to live in. There was so much to eat. Yes, and there were so many kinds of leaves that she liked,—oak, hickory, apple, maple, elm, and several others. Sometimes she wished that she had three mouths instead of one. In those days she had few visitors. It is true that other

Caterpillars happened along once in a while, but they were almost as hungry as she, and they couldn't speak without stopping eating. They could, of course, if they talked with their mouths full, but she had too good manners for that, and, besides, she said that if she did, she couldn't enjoy her food so much.

You must not think that it was wrong in her to care so much about eating. She was only doing what is expected of a Polyphemus Caterpillar, and you would have to do the same if you were a Polyphemus Caterpillar. When she was ten days old she had to weigh ten times as much as she did the morning that she was hatched. When she was twenty days old she had to weigh sixty times as much; when she was a month old she had to weigh six hundred and twenty times as much; and when she was fifty days old she had to weigh four thousand times as much as she did at hatching. Every bit of this flesh was made of the food she ate. That is why eating was so important, you know, and if she had chosen to eat the wrong kind of leaves just because they tasted good, she would never have become such a fine great Caterpillar as she did. She might better not eat anything than to eat the wrong sort, and she knew it.

Still, she often wished that she had more time for visiting, and thought that she would be very gay next year, when she got her wings. "I'll make up for it then," she said to herself, "when my growing is done and I have time for play." Then she ate some more good, plain food, for she knew that there would be no happy Moth-times for Caterpillars who did not eat as they should.

She had five vacations of about a day each when she ate nothing at all. These were the times when she changed her skin, crawling out of the tight old one and appearing as fresh and clean as possible in the new one which was ready underneath. After her last change she was ready to plan her cocoon, and she was a most beautiful Caterpillar. She was about as long as a small cherry leaf, and as plump as a Caterpillar can be. She was light green, with seven slanting yellow lines on each side of her body, and a purplish-brown V-shaped mark on the back part of each side. There were many little orange-colored bunches on her body, which showed beautiful gleaming lights when she moved. Growing out of these bunches were tiny tufts of bristles.

She had three pairs of real legs and several pairs of make-believe ones. Her real legs were on the front part of her body and were slender. These she expected to keep always. The make-believe ones were called pro-legs. They grew farther back and were fat, awkward, jointless things which she would not need after her cocoon was spun. But for them, she would have had to drag the back part of her body around like a Snake. With them, the back part of her body could walk as well as the front, although not quite so fast. She always took a few steps with her real legs and then waited for her pro-legs to catch up.

As the weather grew colder the Polyphemus Caterpillar hunted around on the ground for a good place for her cocoon. She found an excellent twig lying among the dead leaves, and decided to fasten to that. Then began her hardest work, spinning a fluffy mass of gray-white silk which clung to the twig and to one of the dry leaves and was almost exactly the color of the leaf. Other Caterpillars came along and stopped to visit, for they did not have to eat at cocoon-spinning time.

"Better fasten your cocoon to a tree," said a pale bluish-green Promethea Caterpillar. "Put it inside a curled leaf, like mine, and wind silk around the stem to strengthen it. Then you can swing every time the wind blows, and the silk will keep the leaf from wearing out."

"But I don't want to swing," answered the Polyphemus Caterpillar. "I'd rather lie still and think about things."

"Fasten to the twig of a tree," advised a pale green Cecropia Caterpillar with red, yellow, and blue bunches. "Then the wind just moves you a little. Fasten it to a twig and taper it off nicely at each end, and then—"

"Yes," said the Polyphemus Caterpillar, "and then the Blue-Jays and Chickadees will poke wheat or corn or beechnuts into the upper end of it. I don't care to turn my sleeping room into a corn-crib."

Just here some other Polyphemus Caterpillars came along and agreed with their relative. "Go ahead with your tree homes," said they. "We know what we want, and we'll see next summer who knew best."

The Polyphemus cocoons were spun on the ground where the dead leaves had blown in between some stones, and no wandering Cows or Sheep would be likely to step on them. First a mass of coarse silk which it took half a day to make, then an inside coating of a kind of varnish, then as much silk as a Caterpillar could spin in four or five days, next another inside varnishing, and the cocoons were done. As the Polyphemus Caterpillars snuggled down for the long winter's sleep, each said to himself something like this: "Those poor Caterpillars in the trees! How cold they will be! I hope they may come out all right in the spring, but I doubt it very much."

And when the Cecropia and Promethea Caterpillars dozed off for the winter, they said: "What a pity that those Polyphemus Caterpillars would lie around on the ground. Well, we advised them what to do, so it isn't our fault."

They all had a lovely winter, and swung or swayed or lay still, just as they had chosen to do. Early in the spring, the farmer's wife and little girl came out to find wild flowers, and scraped the leaves away from among the stones. Out rolled the cocoon that the first Polyphemus Caterpillar had spun and the farmer's wife picked it up and carried it off. She might have found more cocoons if the little girl had not called her away.

This was how it happened that one May morning a little girl stood by the sitting-room window in the white farmhouse and watched Miss Polyphemus crawl slowly out of her cocoon. A few days before a sour, milky-looking stuff had begun to trickle into the lower end of the cocoon, softening the hard varnish and the soft silken threads until a tiny doorway was opened. Now all was ready and Miss Polyphemus pushed out. She was very wet and weak and forlorn. "Oh," said she to herself, "it is more fun to be a new Caterpillar than it is to be a new Moth. I've only six legs left, and it will be very hard worrying along on these. I shall have to give up walking."

It was discouraging. You can see how it would be. She had been used to having so many legs, and had looked forward all the summer before to the time when she should float lightly through the air and sip honey from flowers. She had dreamed of it all winter. And now here she was—wet and weak, with only six legs left, and four very small and crumpled wings. Her body was so big and fat that she could not hold it up from the window-sill. She wanted to cry—it was all so sad and disappointing. She would have done so, had she not remembered how very unbecoming it is to cry. When she remembered that, she decided to take a nap instead, and that was a most sensible thing to do, for crying always makes matters worse, while sleeping makes them better.

When she awakened, she felt much stronger and more cheerful. She was drier and her body felt

68

lighter. This was because the fluids from it were being pumped into her wings. That was making them grow, and the beautiful colors began to show more brightly on them. "I wonder," she said to herself, "if Moths always feel so badly when they first come out?"

If she had but known it, there were at that very time hundreds of Moths as helpless as she, clinging to branches, leaves, and stones all through the forest. There were many Polyphemus Moths just out, for in their family it is the custom for all to leave their cocoons at just about such a time in the morning. Perhaps she would have felt more patient if she had known this, for it does seem to make hard times easier to bear when one knows that everybody else has hard times also. Of course other people always are having trouble, but she was young and really believed for a time that she was the only uncomfortable Moth in the world.

All day long her wings were stretching and growing smooth. When it grew dark she was nearly ready to fly. Then the farmer's wife lifted her gently by the wings and put her on the inside of the wire window-screen. When the lights in the house were all put out, the moonbeams shone in on Miss Polyphemus and showed her beautiful sand-colored body and wings with the dark border on the front pair and the lighter border on the back pair.

On the back ones were dark eye-spots with clear places in the middle, through which one could see quite clearly.

"I would like to fly," sighed Miss Polyphemus, "and I believe I could if it were not for this horrid screen." She did not know that the farmer's wife had put her there to keep her safe from night birds until she was quite strong.

The wind blew in, sweet with the scent of wild cherry and shad-tree blossoms, and poor Miss Polyphemus looked over toward the forest where she had lived when she was a Caterpillar, and wished herself safely there. "Much good it does me to have wings when I cannot use them," said she. "I want something to eat. There is no honey to be sucked out of wire netting. I wish I were a happy Caterpillar again, eating leaves on the trees." She was not the first Moth who had wished herself a Caterpillar, but she soon changed her mind.

There fluttered toward her another Polyphemus Moth, a handsome fellow, marked exactly as she was, only with darker coloring. His body was more slender, and his feelers were very beautiful and feathery. She was fat and had slender feelers.

"Ah!" said he. "I thought I should find you soon."

"Indeed?" she replied. "I wonder what made you think that?"

"My feelers, of course," said he. "They always tell me where to find my friends. You know how that is yourself."

"I?" said she, as she changed her position a little. "I am just from my cocoon. This was my coming-out day."

"And so you have not met any one yet?" he asked. "Ah, this is a strange world—a very strange world. I would advise you to be very careful with whom you make friends. There are so many bad Moths, you know."

"Good-evening," said a third voice near them, and another Polyphemus Moth with feathery feelers alighted on the screen. He smiled sweetly at Miss Polyphemus and scowled fiercely at the other Moth. It would have ended in a quarrel right then and there, if a fourth Moth had not come at that minute. One after another came, until there were nine handsome fellows on the outside and Miss Polyphemus on the inside of the screen trying to entertain them all and keep them from quarrelling. It made her very proud to think so many were at her coming-out party. Still, she would have enjoyed it better, she thought, if some whom she had known as Caterpillars could be there to see how much attention she was having paid to her. There was one Caterpillar whom she had never liked. She only wished that she could see her now.

Still, society tires one very much, and it was hard to keep her guests from quarrelling. When she got to talking to one about maple-trees, another was sure to come up and say that he had always preferred beech when he was a Caterpillar. And the two

THEY LIVED IN THE FOREST AFTER THAT.

outside would glare at each other while she hastily thought of something else to say.

At last those outside got to fighting. There was only one, the handsomest of all, who said he thought too much of his feelers to fight anybody. "Supposing I should fight and break them off," said he. "I couldn't smell a thing for the rest of my life." He was very sensible, and really the eight other fellows were fighting on account of Miss Polyphemus, for whenever they thought she liked one best they began to bump up against him.

Toward morning the farmer's wife awakened and looked at Miss Polyphemus. When she saw that she was strong enough to fly, she opened the screen and let her go. By that time three of those with feathery feelers were dead, three were broken-winged and clinging helplessly to the screen, and two were so busy fighting that they didn't see Miss Polyphemus go. The handsome great fellow who did not believe in fighting went with her, and they lived in the forest after that. But she never cared for society again.

# THE LONELY OLD BACHELOR MUSKRAT

BEYOND the forest and beside the river lay the marsh where the Muskrats lived. This was the same marsh to which the young Frog had taken some of the meadow people's children when they were tired of staying at home and wanted to travel. When they went with him, you remember, they were gay and happy, the sun was shining, and the way did not seem long. When they came back they were cold and wet and tired, and thought it very far indeed. One could never get them to say much about it.

Some people like what others do not, and one's opinion of a marsh must always depend on whether he is a Grasshopper or a Frog. But whether people cared to live there or not, the marsh had always been a pleasant place to see. In the spring the tall tamaracks along the edge put on their new dresses of soft, needle-shaped green leaves, the marsh-marigolds held their bright faces up to the sun, and hundreds of happy little people darted in and out of the tussocks of coarse grass. There was a warm, wet, earthy smell in the air, and near the pussy-willows there was also a faint bitterness.

Then the Marsh Hens made their nests, and the Sand-pipers ran mincingly along by the quiet pools.

In summer time the beautiful moccasin flowers grew in family groups, and over in the higher, dryer part were masses of white boneset, tall spikes of creamy foxglove, and slender, purple vervain. In the fall the cat-tails stood stiffly among their yellow leaves, and the Red-winged Blackbirds and the Bobolinks perched upon them to plan their journey to the south.

Even when the birds were gone and the cat-tails were ragged and worn—even then, the marsh was an interesting place. Soft snow clung to the brown seed clusters of boneset and filled the open silvery-gray pods of the milkweed. In among the brown tussocks of grass ran the dainty footprints of Mice and Minks, and here and there rose the cone-shaped winter homes of the Muskrats.

The Muskrats were the largest people there, and lived in the finest homes. It is true that if a Mink and a Muskrat fought, the Mink was likely to get the better of the Muskrat, but people never spoke of this, although everybody knew that it was so. The Muskrats were too proud to do so, the Minks were too wise to, and the smaller people who lived near did not want to offend the Muskrats by mentioning it. It is said that an impudent young Mouse did say something about it once when the Muskrats could overhear him and that not one of them ever spoke to him again. The next time he said "Good-evening" to a Muskrat, the Muskrat just looked at him as though he didn't see him or as though he had been a stick or a stone or something else uneatable and uninteresting.

The Muskrats were very popular, for they were kind neighbors and never stole their food from others. That was why nobody was jealous of them, although they were so fat and happy. Their children usually turned out very well, even if they were not at all strictly brought up. You know when a father and mother have to feed and care for fifteen or so children each summer, there is not much time for teaching them to say "please" and "thank you" and "pardon me." Sometimes these young Muskrats did snatch and quarrel, as on that night when fifteen of them went to visit their old home and all wanted to go in first. You may recall how, on that dreadful night, their father had to spank them with his scaly tail and their mother sent them to bed. They always remembered it, and you may be very sure their parents did. It makes parents feel dreadfully when their children quarrel, and it is very wearing to have to spank fifteen at once, particularly when one has to use his tail with which to do it.

There was one old Bachelor Muskrat who had always lived for himself, and had his own way more than was good for him. If he had married, it would not have been so, and he would have grown used to giving up to somebody else. He was a fine-looking fellow with soft, short, reddish-brown fur, which shaded almost to black on his back, and to a light gray underneath. There were very few hairs on his long, flat, scaly tail, and most of these were in two fringes, one down the middle of the upper side, and the other down the middle of the lower side. His tiny ears hardly showed above the fur on his head, and he was so fat that he really seemed to have no neck at all. To look at his feet you would hardly think he could swim, for the webs between his toes were very, very small and his feet were not large.

He was like all other Muskrats in using a great deal of perfume, and it was not a pleasant kind, being so strong and musky. He thought it quite right, and it was better so, for he couldn't help wearing it, and you can just imagine how distressing it would be to see a Muskrat going around with his nose turned up and all the time finding fault with his own perfume.

Nobody could remember the time when there had been no Muskrats in the marsh. The Ground Hog who lived near the edge of the forest said that his grandfather had often spoken of seeing them at play in the moonlight; and there was an old Rattlesnake who had been married several times and wore fourteen joints in his rattle, who said that he remembered seeing Muskrats there before he cast his first skin. And it was not strange that, after their people had lived there so long, the Muskrats should be fond of the marsh.

One day in midsummer the farmer and his men came to the marsh with spades and grub-hoes and measuring lines. All of them had on high rubber boots, and they tramped around and measured and talked, and rooted up a few huckleberry bushes, and drove a good many stakes into the soft and spongy ground. Then the dinner-bell at the farmhouse rang and, they went away. It was a dull, cloudy day and a few of the Muskrats were out. If it had been sunshiny they would have stayed in their burrows. They paddled over to where the stakes were, and smelled of them and gnawed at them, and wondered why the men had put them there.

"I know," said one young Muskrat, who had married and set up a home of his own that spring. "I know why they put these stakes in."

"Oh, do listen!" cried the young Muskrat's wife. "He knows and will tell us all about it."

"Nobody ever told me this," said the young husband. "I thought it out myself. The Ground Hog once said that they put small pieces of potato into the ground to grow into whole big ones, and they have done the same sort of thing here. You see, the farmer wanted a fence, and so he stuck down these stakes, and before winter he will have a fence well grown."

"Humph!" said the Bachelor Muskrat. It seemed as though he had meant to say more, but the young wife looked at him with such a frown on her furry forehead that he shut his mouth as tightly as he could (he never could quite close it) and said nothing else.

"Do you mean to tell me," said one who had just sent five children out of her burrow to make room for another lot of babies, "that they will grow a fence here where it is so wet? Fences grow on high land."

"That is what I said," answered the young husband, slapping his tail on the water to make himself seem more important.

"Well," said the anxious mother, "if they go to growing fences and such things around here I shall move. Every one of my children will want to play around it, and as like as not will eat its roots and get sick."

Then the men came back and all the Muskrats ran toward their burrows, dived into the water to reach the doors of them, and then crawled up the long hallways that they had dug out of the bank until they got to the large rooms where they spent most of their days and kept their babies.

That night the young husband was the first Muskrat to come out, and he went at once to the line of stakes. He had been lying awake and thinking while his wife was asleep, and he was afraid he had talked too much. He found that the stakes had not grown any, and that the men had begun to dig a deep ditch beside them. He was afraid that his neighbors would point their paws at him and ask how the fence was growing, and he was not brave enough to meet them and say that he had been mistaken. He went down to the river bank and fed alone all night, while his wife and neighbors were grubbing and splashing around in the marsh or swimming in the river near their homes. The young Muskrats were rolling and tumbling in the moonlight and looking like furry brown balls. After it began to grow light, he sneaked back to his burrow.

Every day the men came in their high rubber boots to work, and every day there were more ditches and the marsh was drier. By the time that the flowers had all ripened their seeds and the forest trees were bare, the marsh was changed to dry ground, and the Muskrats could find no water there to splash in. One night, and it was a very, very dark one, they came together to talk about winter.

"It is time to begin our cold-weather houses," said one old Muskrat. "I have never started so soon, but we are to have an early winter."

"Yes, and a long one, too," added his wife, who said that Mr. Muskrat never told things quite strongly enough.

"It will be cold," said another Muskrat, "and we shall need to build thick walls."

"Why?" asked a little Muskrat.

"Sh!" said his mother.

"The question is," said the old Muskrat who had first spoken, "where we shall build."

"Why?" asked the little Muskrat, pulling at his mother's tail.

"Sh-h!" said his mother.

"There is no water here except in the ditches," said the oldest Muskrat, "and of course we would not build beside them."

"Why not?" asked the little Muskrat. And this time he actually poked his mother in the side.

"Sh-h-h!" said she. "How many times must I speak to you? Don't you know that young Muskrats should be seen and not heard?"

"But I can't be seen," he whimpered. "It is so dark that I can't be seen, and you've just got to hear me."

Of course, after he had spoken in that way to his mother and interrupted all the others by his naughtiness, he had to be punished, so his mother sent him to bed. That is very hard for young Muskrats, for the night, you know, is the time when they have the most fun.

The older ones talked and talked about what they should do. They knew, as they always do know, just what sort of winter they were to have, and that they must begin to build at once. Some years they had waited until a whole month later, but that was because they expected a late and mild winter. At last the oldest Muskrat decided for them. "We will move to-morrow night," said he. "We will go to the swamp on the other side of the forest and build our winter homes there."

All the Muskrats felt sad about going, and for a minute it was so still that you might almost have heard a milkweed seed break loose from the pod and float away. Then a gruff voice broke the silence. "I will not go," it said. "I was born here and I will live here. I never have left this marsh and I never will leave it."

They could not see who was speaking, but they knew it was the Bachelor. The oldest Muskrat said afterward that he was so surprised you could have knocked him over with a blade of grass. Of course, you couldn't have done it, because he was so fat and heavy, but that is what he said, and it shows just how he felt.

The other Muskrats talked and talked and talked with him, but it made no difference. His brothers told him it was perfectly absurd for him to stay, that people would think it queer, and that he ought to go with the rest of his relatives. Yet it made no difference. "You should stay," he would reply. "Our family have always lived here."

When the Muskrat mothers told him how lonely he would be, and how he would miss seeing the dear little ones frolic in the moonlight, he blinked and said: "Well, I shall just have to stand it." Then he sighed, and they went away saying to each other what a tender heart he had and what a pity it was that he had never married. One of them spoke as though he had been in love with her some years before, but the others had known nothing about it.

The Muskrat fathers told him that he would have no one to help him if a Mink should pick a quarrel with him. "I can take care of myself then," said he, and showed his strong gnawing teeth in a very fierce way.

It was only when the dainty young Muskrat daughters talked to him that he began to wonder if he really ought to stay. He lay awake most of one day thinking about it and remembering the sad look in their little eyes when they said that they should miss him. He was so disturbed that he ate only three small roots during the next night. The poor old Bachelor had a hard time then, but he was so used to having his own way and doing what he had started to do, and not giving up to anybody, that he stayed after all.

The others went away and he began to build his winter house beside the biggest ditch. He placed it among some bushes, so that if the water in the ditch should ever overflow they would help hold his house in place. He built it with his mouth, bringing great mouthfuls of grass roots and rushes and dropping them on the middle of the heap. Sometimes they stayed there and sometimes they rolled down. If they rolled down he never brought them back, for he knew they would be useful where they were. When it was done, the house was shaped like a pine cone with the stem end down, for after he had made it as high as a tall milkweed he finished off the long slope up which he had been running and made it look like the other sides.

After that he began to burrow up into it from below. The right way to do, he knew, was to have his doorway under water and dive down to it. Other winters he had done this and had given the water a loud slap with his tail as he dived. Now there was not enough water to dive into, and when he tried slapping on it his tail went through to the ditch bottom and got muddy. He had to fix the doorway as best he could, and then he ate out enough of the inside of his house to make a good room and poked a small hole through the roof to let in fresh air.

After the house was done, he slept there during the days and prowled around outside at night. He slept there, but ate none of the roots of which it was made until the water in the ditch was frozen hard. He knew that there would be a long, long time when he could not dig fresh roots and must live on those.

At night the marsh seemed so empty and lonely that he hardly knew what to do. He didn't enjoy his meals, and often complained to the Mice that the roots did not taste so good to him as those they used to have when he was young. He tried eating other things and found them no better. When there was bright moonlight, he sat up on the highest tussock he could find and thought about his grandfathers and grandmothers. "If they had not eaten their houses," he once said to a Mouse, "this marsh would be full of them."

"No it wouldn't," answered the Mouse, who didn't really mean to contradict him, but thought him much mistaken. "If the houses hadn't been eaten, they would have been blown down by the wind and beaten down by rains and washed away by

THE MARSH SEEMED SO EMPTY AND LONELY.

floods. It is better so. Who wants things to stay the way they are forever and ever? I'd rather see the trees drop their leaves once in a while and grow new ones than to wear the same old ones after they are ragged and faded."

The Bachelor Muskrat didn't like this very well, but he couldn't forget it. When he awakened in the daytime he would think about it and at night he thought more. He was really very forlorn, and because he had nobody else to think about he thought too much of himself and began to believe that he was lame and sick. When he sat on a tussock and remembered all the houses which his grandparents had built and eaten, he became very sad and sighed until his fat sides shook. He wished that he could sleep through the winter like the Ground Hog, or through part of it like the Skunk, but just as sure as night came his eyes popped open and there he was—awake.

When spring came he thought of his friends who had gone to the swamp and he knew that last year's children were marrying and digging burrows of their own. The poor old Bachelor wanted to go to them, yet he was so used to doing what he had said he would, and disliked so much to let anybody know that he was mistaken, that he chose to stay where he was, without water enough for diving and with hardly enough for swimming. How it would have ended nobody knows, had the farmer not come to plough up the old drained marsh for planting celery.

Then the Bachelor went. He reached his new home in the early morning, and the mothers let their children stay up until it was quite light so that he might see them plainly. "Isn't it pleasant here?" they cried. "Don't you like it better than the old place?"

"Oh, it does very well," he answered, "but you must remember that I only moved because I had to."

"Oh, yes, we understand that," said one of the mothers, "but we hope you will really like it here."

Afterward her husband said to her, "Don't you know he was glad to come? What's the use of being so polite?"

"Poor old fellow," she answered. "He is so queer because he lives alone, and I'm sorry for him. Just see him eat."

And truly it was worth while to watch him, for the roots tasted sweet to him, and, although he had not meant to be, he was very happy—far happier than if he had had his own way.

# THE GREEDY RED FOX

THE Red Fox had been well brought up. His mother was a most cautious person and devoted to her children. When he did things which were wrong, he could never excuse himself by saying that he did not know better. Of course it is possible that he was like his father in being so reckless, yet none of his two brothers and three sisters were like him. They did not remember their father. In fact, they had never seen him, and their mother seldom spoke of him.

His mother had taken all the care of her six children, even pulling fur from her own belly to make a soft nest covering for them when they were first born. They were such helpless babies. Their eyes and ears were closed for some time, and all they could do was to tumble each other around and drink the warm milk that their mother had for them.

They had three burrows to live in, all of them in an open field between the forest and the farmhouse. Sometimes they lived in the first, sometimes in the second, and sometimes in the third. One night when their mother went out to hunt, she smelled along the ground near the burrow and then came back. "There has been a man near here," she said, "and I shall take you away."

That excited the little Foxes very much, and each wanted to be the first to go, but she hushed them up, and said that if they talked so loudly as that some man might catch them before they moved, and then—. She said nothing more, yet they knew from the way she moved her tail that it would be dreadful to have a man catch them.

While she was carrying them to another burrow one at a time, those who were left behind talked about men. "I wish I knew why men are so dreadful," said the first. "It must be because they have very big mouths and sharp teeth."

"I wonder what color their fur is," said another.

Now these young Foxes had seen nobody but their mother. If she had not told them that different animals wore different colored furs, they would have thought that everybody looked just like her, with long reddish-yellow fur and that on the hinder part of the back quite grizzled; throat, belly and the tip of the tail white, and the outside of the ears black. They were very sure, however, that no other animal had such a wonderful tail as she, with each of its long, reddish hairs tipped with black and the beautiful brush of pure white at the end. In fact, she had told them so.

The next time their mother came back, the four children who were still there cried out, "Please tell us, what color is a man's fur?"

She was a sensible and prudent Fox, and knew it was much more important to keep her children from being caught than it was to answer all their questions at once. Besides, she already had one child in her mouth when they finished their question, and she would not put him down for the sake of talking. And that also was right, you know, for one can talk at any time, but the time to do work is just when it needs to be done.

After they were snugly settled in the other burrow, she lay down to feed them, and while they were drinking their milk she told them about men. "Men," she said, "are the most dreadful animals there are. Other animals will not trouble you unless they are hungry, but a man will chase you even when his stomach is full. They have four legs, of course,— all animals have,—but they use only two to walk upon. Their front legs they use for carrying things. We carry with our mouths, yet the only thing I ever saw a man have in his mouth was a short brown stick that was afire at one end. I thought it very silly, for he couldn't help breathing some of the smoke, and he let the stick burn up and then threw the fire away. However, men are exceedingly silly animals."

One of the little Red Foxes stopped drinking long enough to say, "You didn't tell us what color their fur is."

"The only fur they have," said Mother Fox, "is on their heads. They usually have fur on the top and back parts of their heads, and some of them have a little on the lower part of their faces. They may have black, red, brown, gray, or white fur. It is never spotted."

The children would have liked to ask more questions, but Mother Fox had eaten nothing since the night before, and was in a hurry to begin her hunt.

One could never tell all that happened to the little Red Foxes. They moved from burrow to burrow many times; they learned to eat meat which their mother brought them instead of drinking milk from her body, they frolicked together near the doorway of their home, and while they did this their mother watched from the edge of the forest, ready to warn them if she saw men or dogs coming.

She had chosen to dig her burrows in the middle of a field, because then there was no chance for men or Dogs to sneak up to them unseen, as there would have been in the forest, yet she feared that her children would be playing so hard that they might forget to watch. They slept most of the day, and at night they were always awake. When they were old enough, they began to hunt for themselves. Mother Fox gave them a great deal of good advice and then paid no more attention to them. After that, she took her naps on a sunny hillside, lying in a beautiful soft reddish-yellow bunch, with her bushy tail curled around to keep her feet warm and shade her eyes from the light.

The six brothers and sisters seldom saw each other after this. Foxes succeed better in life if they live alone, and of course they wanted to succeed. The eldest brother was the reckless one. His mother had done her best by him, and still he was reckless. He knew by heart all the rules that she had taught him, but he did not keep them. These were the rules:

"Always run on hard, dry things when you can. Soft, wet places take more scent from your feet, and Dogs can follow your trail better on them.

"Never go into any place unless you are sure you can get out.

"Keep your tail dry. A Fox with a wet tail cannot run well.

"If Dogs are chasing you, jump on to a rail fence and run along the top of it or walk in a brook.

"Always be willing to work for your food. That which you find all ready and waiting for you may be the bait of a trap.

"Always walk when you are hunting. The Fox who trots will pass by that which he should find."

For a while he said them over to himself every night when he started out. Then he began to skip a night once in a while. Next he got to saying them only when he had been frightened the day before. After that he stopped saying them altogether. "I am a full-grown Fox now," he said to himself, "and such things are only good for children. I guess I know how to take care of myself."

He often went toward the farmhouse to hunt, sometimes for grapes, sometimes for vegetables, and sometimes for heartier food. Collie had chased him away, but Collie was growing old and fat and had to hang his tongue out when he ran, so the Red Fox thought it only fun. He trotted along in the moonlight, his light, slender body seeming to almost float over the ground, and his beautiful tail held straight out behind. His short, slender legs were strong and did not tire easily, and as long as he could keep his tail dry he outran Collie easily. Sometimes he would get far ahead and sit down to wait for him. Then he would call out saucy things to the panting Dog, and only start on when Collie's nose had almost touched him.

"Fine evening!" he once said. "Hope your nose works better than your legs do."

That was a mean thing to say, you know, but Collie always kept his temper and only answered, "It's sweating finely, thank you." He answered that way because it is the sweat on a Dog's nose which makes it possible for him to smell and follow scents which dry-nosed people do not even know about.

Then the Fox gave a long, light leap, and was off again, and Collie had to lie down to breathe. "I think," said he, "that I can tend Sheep better than I can chase Foxes—and it is a good deal easier." Still, Collie didn't like to be beaten and he lay awake the rest of the night thinking how he would enjoy catching that Fox. Every little while he heard the Red Fox barking off in the fields, and it made him twitch his tail with impatience.

Now the Red Fox was walking carefully toward the farmhouse and planning to catch a Turkey. He had watched the flocks of Turkeys all afternoon from his sleeping-place on the hillside. Every time he opened his eyes between naps he had looked at them as they walked to and fro in the fields, talking to each other in their gentle, complaining voices and moving their heads back and forth at every step. If his stomach had not been so full he would have tried to catch one then. He made up his mind to try it that night, and decided that he would rather have the plump, light-colored one than any of her darker sisters. He did not even think of catching the old Gobbler, for he was so big and strong and fierce-looking. He had just begun to walk with the Turkey mothers and children. During the summer they had had nothing to do with each other.

When the Red Fox reached the farmyard, he found them roosting on the low branches of an apple-tree. A long board had been placed against it to let the Chickens walk up. Now the Chickens were in the Hen-house, but the board was still there. The Red Fox looked all around. It was a starlight night. The farmhouse was dark and quiet. Collie was nowhere to be seen. Once he heard a Horse stamp in his sleep. Then all was still again.

The Red Fox walked softly up the slanting board. The Gobbler stirred. The Red Fox stopped with one foot in the air. When he thought him fast asleep he went on. The Gobbler stirred again and so did the others. The Red Fox sprang for the plump, light-colored one. She jumped also, and with the others flew far up to the top of the barn. The Red Fox ran down the board with five buff tail-feathers in his mouth. He was much out of patience with himself. "If I hadn't stopped to pick for her," he said, "I could have caught one of the others easily enough."

He sneaked around in the shadows to see if the noise made by the turkeys had awakened the farmer or Collie. The farmhouse was still and dark. Collie was not at home. "I will look at the Hen-house," said the Red Fox.

He walked slowly and carefully to the Hen-house. The big door was closed and bolted. He walked all around and into the poultry yard. There was a small opening through which the fowls could pass in and out. The Red Fox managed to crawl through, but it was not easy. It squeezed his body and crushed his fur. He had to push very hard with his hind feet to get through at all. When he was inside it took him some time to get his breath. "That's the tightest place I ever was in," said he softly, "but I always could crawl through a very small hole."

He found the fowls all roosting too high for him. Perhaps if the Hen-house had been larger, he might have leaped and caught one, but there was not room for one of his finest springs. He went to the nests and found many eggs there. These he broke and ate. They ran down in yellow streams from the corners of his mouth and made his long fur very sticky. You can just imagine how hard it would be to eat raw eggs from the shell with only your paws in which to hold them.

One egg was light and slippery. He bit hard to break that one, and when it broke it was hollow. Not a drop of anything to eat in it, and then it cut his lip a little, too, so that he could not eat more without its hurting. He jumped and said something when he was cut. The Shanghai Cock, who was awakened by the noise, said that he exclaimed, "Brambles and traps!" but it may not have been anything so bad as that. We will hope it was not.

The Shanghai Cock awakened all the other fowls. "Don't fly off your perch!" he cried. "Stay where you are! *Stay where you are!* STAY WHERE YOU ARE!" The other Cocks kept saying "Eru-u-u-u," as they do when Hawks are near. The Hens squawked and squawked and squawked until they were out of breath. When they got their breath they squawked some more.

The Red Fox knew that it was time for him to go. The farmer would be sure to hear the noise. He put his head out of the hole through which he had come in, and he pushed as hard as he could with his hind feet and scrambled with his fore feet. His fur was crushed worse than ever, and he was squeezed so tightly that he could hardly breathe. You see it had been all he could do to get in through the hole, and now he had nine eggs in his stomach (excepting what had run down at the corners of his mouth), and he was too large to pass through.

The fowls saw what was the matter, and wanted to laugh. They thought it was very funny, and yet the sooner he could get away the better they would like it. The Red Fox had his head outside and saw a light flash in the farmer's room. Then he heard doors open, and the farmer came toward the Hen-house with a lantern in his hand. Collie came trotting around the corner of the house. The Red Fox made one last desperate struggle and then lay still.

When the farmer picked him up and tied a rope around his neck, he had to pull him backward into the Hen-house to do it. The Red Fox was very quiet and gentle, as people of his family always are when caught. Collie pranced around on two legs and barked as loudly as he could. The fowls blinked their round yellow eyes in the lantern light, and the farmer's man ran out for an empty Chicken-coop into which to put the Red Fox. Collie was usually quite polite, but he had not forgotten how rude the Red Fox had been to him, and it was a fine chance to get even.

"Good evening!" he barked. "Oh, good evening! I'm glad you came. Don't think you must be going. Excuse me, but your mouth worked better than your legs, didn't it?"

The Red Fox shut his eyes and pretended not to hear. The dirt from the floor of the Hen-house had stuck to his egg-covered fur, and he looked very badly. They put him in a Chicken-coop with a board floor, so that he couldn't burrow out, and he curled down in a little heap and hid his face with his tail. Collie hung around for a while and then went off to sleep. After he was gone, the Red Fox cleaned his fur. "I got caught this time," he said, "but it won't happen again. Now I must watch for a chance to get away. It will surely come."

It did come. But that is another story.

# THE UNFORTUNATE
# FIREFLIES

S EVERAL very large families of Fireflies lived in the marsh and were much admired by their friends who were awake at night. Once in a while some young Firefly who happened to awaken during the day would go out and hover over the heads of the daylight people. He never had any attention paid to him then, however, for during the day he seemed like a very commonplace little beetle and nobody even cared to look at him a second time. The only remarkable thing about him was the soft light that shone from his body, and that could only be seen at night.

The older Fireflies told the younger ones that they should get all the sleep they could during the daytime if they were to flutter and frisk all night. Most of them did this, but two young Fireflies, who cared more about seeing the world than they did about minding their elders, used to run away while the rest were dreaming. Each thought herself very important, and was sure that if the others missed her they wouldn't sleep a wink all day.

One night they planned to go by daylight to the farthest corner of the marsh. They had heard a couple of young Muskrats talking about it, and thought it might be different from anything they had seen. They went to bed when the rest did and pretended to fall asleep. When she was sure that the older Fireflies were dreaming, one of them reached over with her right hind leg and touched the other just below the edge of her left wing-cover. "Are you ready?" she whispered.

"Yes," answered the friend, who happened to be the smaller of the two.

"Come on, then," said the larger one, picking her way along on her six tiptoes. It was already growing light, and they could see where they stepped, but, you know, it is hard to walk over rough places on two tiptoes, so you can imagine what it must be on six. There are some pleasant things about having so many legs. There are also some hard things. It is a great responsibility.

When well away from their sleeping relatives, they lifted their wing-covers, spread their wings, and flew to the farthest corner of the marsh. They were not afraid of being punished if caught, for they were orphans and had nobody to bring them up. They were afraid that if the other Fireflies awakened they would be called "silly" or "foolish young bugs." They thought that they were old enough to take care of themselves, and did not want advice.

"Oh, wouldn't they make a fuss if they knew!" exclaimed the Larger Firefly.

"They think we need to be told every single thing," said the Smaller Firefly.

"Guess we're old enough now to go off by ourselves," said the Larger Firefly.

"I guess so," answered the Smaller Firefly. "I'm not afraid if it is light, and I can see pretty near as well as I can at night."

Just then a Flycatcher darted toward them and they had to hide. He had come so near that they could look down his throat as he flew along with his beak open. The Fireflies were so scared that their feelers shook.

"I wish that bird would mind his own business," grumbled the Larger Firefly.

"That's just what he was doing," said a voice beside them, as a Garter Snake drew himself through the grass. Then their feelers shook again, for they knew that snakes do not breakfast on grass and berries.

"Did you ever see such luck?" said the Smaller Firefly. "If it isn't birds it is snakes."

"Perfectly dreadful!" answered the other. "I never knew the marsh to be so full of horrid people. Besides, my eyes are bothering me and I can't see plainly."

"So are mine," said the Smaller Firefly. "Are you going to tell the other Fireflies all about things to-night?"

"I don't know that I will," said the Larger Firefly. "I'll make them ask me first."

Then they reached the farther corner of the marsh and crawled around to see what they could find. Their eyes bothered them so that they could not see unless they were close to things, so it was useless to fly. They peeped into the cool dark corners under the skunk cabbage leaves, and lay down to rest on a bed of soft moss. A few stalks of last year's teazles stood, stiff and brown, in the corner of the fence. The Smaller Firefly alighted on one and let go in such a hurry that she fell to the ground. "Ouch!" she cried. "It has sharp hooks all over it."

While they were lying on the moss and resting, they noticed a queer plant growing near. It had a flower of green and dark red which was unlike any other blossom they had ever seen. The leaves were even queerer. Each was stiff and hollow and grew right out of the ground instead of coming from a stalk.

"I'm going to crawl into one of them," said the Larger Firefly. "There is something sweet inside. I believe it will be lots better than the skunk cabbage." She balanced herself on the top of a fresh green leaf.

"I'm going into this one," said the other Firefly, as she alighted on the edge of a brown-tipped leaf. "It looks nice and dark inside. We must tell about this at the party to-night, even if they don't ask us."

Then they repeated together the little verse that some of the pond people use when they want to start together:

"Tussock, mud, water, and log,
Muskrat, Snake, Turtle, and Frog,
Here we go into the bog!"

When they said "bog" each dropped quickly into her own leaf.

For a minute nobody made a sound. Then there was a queer sputtering, choking voice in the fresh green leaf and exactly the same in the brown-tipped one. After that a weak little voice in the green leaf said, "Abuschougerh! I fell into water."

Another weak voice from the brown-tipped one replied, "Gtschagust! So did I."

On the inside of each leaf were many stiff hairs, all pointing downward. When the Fireflies dropped in, they had brushed easily past these hairs and thought it rather pleasant. Now that they were sputtering and choking inside, and wanted to get out, these same hairs stuck into their eyes and pushed against their legs and made them exceedingly uncomfortable. The water, too, had stood for some time in the leaves and did not smell good.

Perhaps it would be just as well not to tell all the things which those two Fireflies said, for they were tired and out of patience. After a while they gave up trying to get out until they should be rested. It was after sunset when they tried the last time, and the light that shone from their bellies brightened the little green rooms where they were. They rested and went at it carefully, instead of in the angry, jerky way which they had tried before. Slowly, one foot at a time, they managed to climb out of the doorway at the top. As they came out, they heard the squeaky voice of a young Mouse say, "Oh, where did those bright things come from?"

They also heard his mother answer, "Those are only a couple of foolish Fireflies who have been in the leaves of the pitcher-plant all day."

After they had eaten something they flew toward home. They knew that it would be late for the party, and they expected to surprise and delight everybody when they reached there. On the way they spoke of this. "I'm dreadfully tired," said one, "but I suppose we shall have to dance in the air with the rest or they will make a fuss."

"Yes," said the other. "It spoils everything if we are not there. And we'll have to tell where we've been and what we've done and whom we have seen, when we would rather go to sleep and make up what we lost during the daytime."

As they came near the middle of the marsh they were surprised to see the mild summer air twinkling with hundreds of tiny lights as their friends and relatives flew to and fro in the dusk. "Well," said the Larger Firefly, "I think they might have waited for us!"

"Humph!" said the Smaller Firefly. "If they can't be more polite than that, I won't play."

104

TWINKLING WITH HUNDREDS OF TINY LIGHTS.

"After we've had such a dreadfully hard time, too," said the Larger Firefly. "Got most eaten by a Flycatcher and scared by a Garter Snake and shut up all day in the pitcher-plant. I won't move a wing to help on their old party."

So two very tired and cross young Fireflies sat on a last year's cat-tail and sulked. People didn't notice them because they were sitting and their bright bellies didn't show. After a long time an elderly Firefly came to rest on the cat-tail and found them. "Good evening," said he. "Have you danced until you are tired?"

They looked at each other, but before either could speak one of their young friends alighted beside them and said the same thing. Then the Smaller Firefly answered. "We have been away," said she, "and we are not dancing tonight."

"Going away, did you say?" asked the elderly Firefly, who was rather deaf. "I hope you will have a delightful time." Then he bowed and flew off.

"Don't stay long," added their young friend. "We shall be so lonely without you."

After he also was gone, the two runaways looked into each other's eyes. "We were not even missed!" they cried. "We had a bad time and nobody makes any fuss. They were dancing without us." Poor little Fireflies!

They were much wiser after that, for they had learned that two young Fireflies were not so wonderfully important after all. And that if they chose to do things which it was never meant young Fireflies should do, they would be likely to have a very disagreeable time, but that other Fireflies would go on eating and dancing and living their own lives. To be happy, they must keep the Firefly laws.

# THE KITTENS COME TO THE FOREST

ONE day the three big Kittens who lived with their mother in the farmer's barn had a dreadful quarrel. If their mother had been with them, she would probably have cuffed each with her fore paw and scolded them soundly. She was not with them because she had four little new Kittens lying beside her in the hay-loft over the stalls.

You would think that the older Kittens must have been very proud of their baby brothers and sisters, yet they were not. They might have done kind little things for their mother, but they didn't. They just hunted food for themselves and never took a mouthful of it to her. And this does not prove that they were bad Kittens. It just shows that they were young and thoughtless.

The Brown Kitten, the one whose fur was black and yellow mixed so finely as to look brown, had climbed the barn stairs to see them. When he reached their corner he sat down and growled at them. His mother said nothing at first, but when he went so far as to switch his tail in a threatening way, she left her new babies and sprang at him and told him not to show his whiskers upstairs again until he could behave properly.

His sisters, the Yellow Kitten and the White Kitten, stayed downstairs. They didn't dislike babies so much as their brother. They just didn't care anything about them. Cats never care much about Kittens, you know, unless they are their own, and big brothers always say that they can't bear them.

Now these three older Kittens were perfectly able to care for themselves. It was a long time since their mother stopped feeding them, and they were already excellent hunters. They had practiced crouching, crawling, and springing before they left the hay-loft. Sometimes they hunted wisps of hay that moved when the wind blew in through the open door. Sometimes they pounced on each other, and sometimes they hunted the Grasshoppers who got brought in with the hay. It was when they were doing this once that they were so badly scared, but that is a story which has already been told.

There was no reason why they should feel neglected or worry about getting enough to eat. If one of them had poor luck in hunting, all he had to do was to hang around the barn when the Cows were brought up, and go into the house with the man when he carried the great pails full of foamy milk. Then if the Kittens acted hungry, mewed very loudly, and rubbed up lovingly against the farmer's wife they were sure to get a good dishful of warm milk.

You can see how unreasonable they were. They had plenty to eat, and their mother loved them just as much as ever, but they felt hurt and sulked around in corners, and answered each other quite rudely, and would not run after a string which the farmer's little girl dangled before them. They were not cross all the time, because they had been up the whole night and had to sleep. They stopped being cross when they fell asleep and began again as soon as they awakened. The Hens who were feeding around became so used to it that as soon as they saw a Kitten twist and squirm, and act like awakening, they put their heads down and ran away as fast as they could.

They did not even keep themselves clean. Oh, they licked themselves over two or three times during the day, but not thoroughly. The Yellow Kitten did not once try to catch her tail and scrub it, and actually wore an unwashed tail all day. It didn't show very plainly because it was yellow, but that made it no cleaner. The White Kitten went around with her fore paws looking really disgraceful. The Brown Kitten scrubbed his ears in a sort of half-hearted way, and paid no attention to the place under his chin. When he did his ears, he gave his paw one lick and his ear one rub, and repeated this only six times. Everybody knows that a truly tidy Cat wets his paw with two licks, cleans his ear with two rubs, and does this over and over from twenty to forty times before he begins on the other ear.

Toward night they quarreled over a dishful of milk which the farmer's wife gave them. There was plenty of room for them all to put their heads into the dish at once and lap until each had his share. If it had not been for their whiskers, there would have been no trouble. These hit, and each told the others to step back and wait. Nobody did, and there was such a fuss that the farmer's wife took the dish away and none of them had any more. They began to blame each other and talk so loudly that the man drove them all away as fast as they could scamper.

Now that they were separated, each began to grow more and more discontented. The Brown Kitten had crawled under the carriage house, and as soon as it was really dark he stole off to the forest.

"My mother has more Kittens," he said, "and my sisters get my whiskers all out of shape, and I'll go away and never come back. I won't say good-bye to them either. I guess they'll feel badly then and wish they'd been nicer to me! If they ever find me and want me to come back, I won't go. Not if they beg and beg! I'll just turn my tail toward them and walk away."

The Brown Kitten knew that Cats sometimes went to live in the woods and got along very well. He was not acquainted with one who had done this; his mother had told him and his sisters stories of Cats who chose to live so. She said that was one thing which showed how much more clever they were than Dogs. Dogs, you know, cannot live happily away from men, although there may be the best of hunting around them.

"I will find a good hollow tree," said he, "for my home, and I will sleep there all day and hunt at night. I will eat so much that I shall grow large and strong. Then, when I go out to hunt, the forest people will say, 'Sh! Here comes the Brown Cat.' "

As he thought this he was running softly along the country road toward the forest. Once in a while he stopped to listen, and stood with his head raised and turned and one fore foot in the air. He kept his ears pointed forward all the time so as to hear better.

When he passed the marsh he saw the Fireflies dancing in the air. Sometimes they flew so low that a Kitten might catch them. He thought he would try, so he crawled through the fence and toward the place where they were dancing. He passed two tired ones sitting on a leaf and never saw them. That was because their wings covered their sides so well that no light shone past, and their bright bellies were close to the leaf. He had almost reached the dancers when he found his paws getting wet and muddy. That made him turn back at once, for mud was something he couldn't stand. "I wish I had something to eat," he said, as he took a bite of catnip. "This is very good for a relish, but not for a whole meal."

He trotted on toward the forest, thinking about milk and Fireflies and several other things, when he was stopped by some great winged person flying down toward him and then sweeping upward and alighting on a branch. The Brown Kitten drew back stiffly and said, "Ha-a-ah!"

"Who? Who? To who?" asked the person on the branch.

The Brown Kitten answered, "It is I." But the question came again: "Who? Who? To who?"

That made the Brown Kitten remember that, since his voice was not known in the forest, nobody could tell anything by his answer. This time he replied: "I am the Brown Kitten, if you please, and I have come to live in the forest."

"Who? Who? To who?" was the next question, and the Brown Kitten thought he was asked to whose home he was going.

"I am not going to anybody," he said. "I just wanted to come, and left my old home suddenly. I shall live alone and have a good time. I didn't even tell my mother."

"Who? Who? To who?" said the Great Horned Owl, for it was he.

"My m-mother," said the Brown Kitten, and then he ran away as fast as he could. He had seen the Owl more clearly as he spoke, and the Owl's face reminded him a little of his mother and made him want to see her. He ran so fast that he almost bumped into the Skunk, who was taking a dignified stroll through the forest and sniffing at nearly everything he saw. It was very lucky, you know, that he did not quite run into the Skunk, for Skunks do

113

not like to be run into, and, if he had done so, other people would soon have been sniffing at him.

The Brown Kitten thought that the Skunk might be related to him. They were about the same size, and the Brown Kitten had been told that his relatives were not only different colors, but different shapes. His mother had told of seeing some Manx Kittens who had no tails at all, and he thought that the Skunk's elegant long-haired one needn't prevent his being a Cat.

"Good evening," said the Brown Kitten. "Would you mind telling me if you are a Cat?"

"Cat? No!" growled the Skunk. "They sometimes call me a Wood-Kitty, but they have no right to. I am a Skunk, *Skunk*, SKUNK, and I am related to the Weasels. Step out of my path."

A family of young Raccoons in a tree called down teasingly to him to come up, but after he had started they told him to go down, and then laughed at him because he had to go tail first. He did not know that forest climbers turn the toes of their hind feet backward and scamper down head first. Still, it would have made no difference if he had known, for his toes wouldn't turn.

He found something to eat now and then, and he looked for a hollow tree. He found only one, and that was a Bee tree, so he couldn't use it. All around him the most beautiful mushrooms were pushing up from the ground. White, yellow, orange, red, and brown they were, and looked so plump and fair that he wanted to bite them. He knew, however, that some of them were very poisonous, so he didn't even lick them with his eager, rough little pink tongue. He was just losing his Kitten teeth, and his new Cat teeth were growing, and they made him want to bite almost everything he saw. One kind of mushroom, which he thought the prettiest of all, grew only on the trunks of fallen beech trees. It was white, and had a great many little branches, all very close together.

Most of the plants he saw were sound asleep. Every plant has to sleep, you know, and most of them take a long nap at night. Some of them, like the water-lilies, also sleep on cloudy days. He was very fond of the clovers, but they had their leaflets folded tight, and only the mushrooms, the evening primroses, and a few others were wide awake. Everybody whom he met was a stranger, and he began to feel very lonely. Cats do not usually mind being alone. Indeed, they rather like it; still, you can see how hard it would be for a Kitten who had always been loved and cared for to find himself alone in a dark forest, where great birds ask the same questions over and over, and other people make fun of him. You wouldn't like it yourself, if you were a Kitten.

At last, when he was prowling along an old forest road and hoping to meet a tender young Wood-Mouse, he saw a couple of light-colored animals ahead of him. They looked to him very much like Kittens, but he remembered how the Skunk had snubbed him when taken for a Cat, and he kept still. He ran to overtake them and see more clearly, and just as he reached them they all came to a turn in the road.

Before he could speak or they could notice that he was there, the wind roared through the branches above, and just ahead two terrible great eyes glared at them out of an old log. They all stopped with their back-fur bristling and their tails arched stiffly. Not a sound did one of them make. They lifted first one foot and then another and backed slowly and silently away. When they had gone far enough, they turned quickly and ran down the old road as fast as their twelve feet could carry them. They never stopped until they were in the road for home and could look back in the starlight and be sure that nobody was following them. Then they stared at each other—the Yellow Kitten, the White Kitten, and the Brown Kitten.

"Did you run away to live in the forest?" asked the sisters.

"Did you?" asked the Brown Kitten.

"You'll never tell?" said they.

"Never!" said he.

"Well then, we did run away, and met each other just before you came. We meant to live in the forest."

"So did I," said he. "And I couldn't find any hollow tree."

"Did you meet that dreadful bird?" said they,—"the one who never hears your answers and keeps asking you over and over?"

"Yes," said he. "Don't you ever tell!"

"Ha-ha!" screamed a laughing little Screech-Owl, who had seen what had happened in the old forest road and flapped along noiselessly behind them. "Three big Kittens afraid of fox-fire! O-ho! O-ho!"

Now all of them had heard about fox-fire and knew it was the light which shines from some kinds of rotten wood in the dark, but they held up their heads and answered, "We're not afraid of fox-fire."

"Ha-ha!" screamed the Screech-Owl again. "Thought you saw big eyes glaring at you. Only fox-fire. Dare you to come back if you are not afraid."

"We don't want to go back," answered the Brown Kitten. "We haven't time."

"Ha-ha!" screamed the Screech-Owl again. "Haven't time! Where are you going?"

"Going home, of course," answered the Brown Kitten. And then he whispered to his sisters, "Let's!"

"All right," said they, and they raced down the road as fast as they could go. To this day their mother does not know that they ever ran away from home.

But it was only fox-fire.

# THE INQUISITIVE WEASELS

T HE Weasels were very unpopular with most of the forest people, the pond and meadow people did not like them, and those who lived in the farmyard couldn't bear them. Something went wrong there every time that a Weasel came to call. Once, you know, the Dorking Hen was so frightened that she broke her wonderful shiny egg, and there were other times when even worse things had happened. Usually there was a Chicken or two missing after the Weasel had gone.

The Weasels were very fond of their own family, however, and would tell their best secrets to each other. That meant almost as much with them as to share food, for they were very inquisitive and always wanted to know all about everything. They minded their own business, but they minded everybody's else as well. If you told a thing to one Weasel you might be sure that before the night was over every Weasel in the neighborhood would know all about it. They told other people, too, when they had a chance. They were dreadful gossips. If they saw a person do something the least unusual, they thought about it and talked about it and wondered what it meant, and decided that it meant something very remarkable and became very much excited. At such times, they made many excuses to go calling, and always managed to tell about what they had seen, what they had heard, and what they were perfectly certain it meant.

They went everywhere, and could go quietly and without being noticed. They were small people, about as long as Rats, but much more slender, and with such short legs that their bodies seemed to almost lie on the ground. All their fur was brown, except that on their bellies and the inside of their legs, which was pure white. Sometimes the fur on their feet matched their backs and sometimes it matched their bellies. That was as might happen. You can easily see how they could steal along over the brown earth or the dead leaves and grass without showing plainly. In winter they turned white, and then they did not show on the snow. The very tip of their short tails stayed a pale brown, but it was so tiny as hardly to be noticed. Any Hawk in the air, who saw just that bit of brown on the snow beneath him, would be likely to think it a leaf or a piece of bark and pay no more attention to it.

The Weasel mothers were very careful of their children and very brave. It made no difference how great the danger might be, they would stay by their babies and fight for them. And such workers as they were! It made no difference to them whether it was day or night, they would burrow or hunt just the

IN WINTER THEY TURNED WHITE.

same. When they were tired they slept, and when they awakened they began at once to do something.

Several families lived in the high bank by the edge of the forest, just where the ground slopes down to the marsh. They had lived there year after year, and had kept on adding to their burrows. There was only one doorway to each burrow and that was usually hidden by some leaves or a stone. They were hardly as large as Chipmunk's holes and easily hidden. "It is a good thing to have a fine, large home," said the Weasels, "but we build for comfort, not for show."

All the Weasel burrows began alike, with a straight, narrow hall. Then more halls branched off from this, and every little way there would be a room in which to turn around or rest. In some of these they stored food; in others they had nothing but bones and things which were left from their meals. Each burrow had one fine, large room, bigger than an Ovenbird's nest, with a soft bed of leaves and fur. Some of the rooms were so near the top of the ground that a Weasel could dig his way up in a few minutes if he needed another door. They were the loveliest sort of places for playing hide-and-seek, and that is a favorite Weasel game, only every Weasel wants to seek instead of hiding. There was never a bit of loose earth around these homes, and that is the one secret which Weasels will not tell out of the family—they never tell what they do with the earth they dig out. It just disappears.

Weasels like to hunt in parties. They say there is no fun in doing anything unless you have somebody with whom to talk it over. One night four of them went out together as soon as it was dark. They were young fellows and had planned to go to the farmer's Hen-house for the first time. They started to go there, but of course they wanted to see everything by the way. They would run straight ahead for a little while, then turn off to one side, as Ants do, poking into a Chipmunk's hole or climbing a tree to find a bird's nest, eating whatever food they found, and talking softly about everything.

"It is disgraceful the way that Chipmunk keeps house," said one of them, as he came back from going through a burrow under a tree. "Half-eaten food dropped right on the floor of the burrow in the most careless way. It was only a nut. If it had been anything I cared for, I would have eaten it myself."

Then they gossiped about Chipmunks, and said that, although they always looked trim and neat, there was no telling what sort of housekeepers they were; and that it really seemed as though they would do better to stay at home more and run about the forest less. The Chipmunk heard all this from the tree where he had hidden himself, and would have liked to speak right out and tell them what he thought of callers who entered one's home without knocking and sneaked around to see how things were kept. He knew better than to do so, however. He knew that when four hungry Weasels were out hunting their supper, it was an excellent time to keep still. He was right. And there are many times when it is better for angry people to keep still, even if they are not afraid of being eaten.

After they had gone he came down. "It was lucky for me," he said, "that I awakened hungry and ate a lunch. If I hadn't been awake to run away there's no telling where I would be now. There are some things worse than having people think you a poor housekeeper."

Just as the Chipmunk was finishing his lunch, one of the Weasels whispered to the others to stop. "There is somebody coming," said he. "Let's wait and see what he is doing."

It was the Black-tailed Skunk, who came along slowly, sniffing here and there, and once in a while stopping to eat a few mouthfuls.

"Doesn't it seem to you that he acts very queerly?" said one of the Weasels to the rest.

"Very," replied another. "And he doesn't look quite as usual. I don't know that I ever saw him carry his tail in just that way."

"I'd like to know where he is going," said another. "I guess he doesn't think anybody will see him."

"Let's follow him," said the fourth Weasel, who had not spoken before.

While he was near them they hid behind a hemlock log out of which many tiny hemlocks were growing. Once in a while they peeped between the soft fringy leaves of these to see what he was doing.

They were much excited. "He is putting his nose down to the ground," one would say. "It must be that he has found something."

Then another would poke his little head up through the hemlocks and look at the Skunk. "He couldn't have found anything after all," he would say. "I can't hear him eating."

"It is very strange," the rest would murmur.

Now it just happened that the Black-tailed Skunk had scented the Weasels and knew that they were near. He had also heard the rustling behind the hemlock log. He knew what gossips Weasels are, and he guessed that they were watching him, so he decided to give them something to think about. He knew that they would often fight people larger than themselves, but he was not afraid of anybody. He did not care to fight them either, for if he got near enough to really enjoy it they would be likely to bite him badly, and when a Weasel has set his teeth into anybody it is not easy to make him let go. "I rather think," said he to himself, "that there will be four very tired young Weasels sleeping in their burrows to-morrow."

"He's walking away," whispered one of the Weasels. "Where do you suppose he is going?"

"We'll have to find out," said the others, as they crept quietly out of their hiding-places.

The Skunk went exactly where he wanted to. Whenever he found food he ate it. The Weasels who followed after found nothing left for them. They became very hungry, but if one of them began to think of going off for a lunch, the Skunk was certain to do something queer. Sometimes he would lie down and laugh. Then the Weasels would peep at him from a hiding-place and whisper together.

"What do you suppose makes him laugh?" they would ask. "It must be that he is thinking of something wonderful which he is going to do. We must not lose sight of him."

Once he met the Spotted Skunk, his brother, and they whispered together for a few minutes. Then the Spotted Skunk laughed, and as he passed on, the Black-tailed Skunk called back to him: "Be sure not to tell any one. I do not want it known what I am doing."

Then the four young Weasels nudged each other and said, "There! We knew it all the time!"

After that, nobody spoke about being hungry. All they cared for was the following of the Black-tailed Skunk. Once, when they were in the marsh, they were so afraid of being seen that they slipped into the ditch and swam for a way. They were good swimmers and didn't much mind, but it just shows how they followed the Skunk. Once he led them over to the farm and they remembered their plan of going to the Hen-house. They were very, very hungry, and each looked at the others to see what they thought about letting the Skunk go and stopping for a hearty supper. Still, nobody spoke of doing so. One Weasel whispered: "Now we shall surely see what he is about. He ought to know that he cannot do wrong or mischievous things without being found out. And since we discover it ourselves, we shall certainly feel free to speak of it."

Collie, the watch-dog, was sleeping lightly, and came rushing around the corner of the house to see what strangers were there, but when he saw who they were, he dropped his tail and walked away. He was old enough to know many things, and he knew too much to fight either a Skunk or a Weasel. Every one lets Skunks alone, and it is well to let Weasels alone also, for although they are so small they bite badly.

Now the Black-tailed Skunk turned to the forest and walked toward his hole. The Screech-Owl passed them flying homeward, and several times Bats darted over their heads. When they went by the Bats' cave they could tell by the sound that ten or twelve were inside hanging themselves up for the day. A dim light showed in the eastern sky, and the day birds were stirring and beginning to preen their feathers.

"What do you think it means?" whispered the Weasels. "He seems to be going home. Do you suppose he has changed his mind?"

When he reached his hole, the Black-tailed Skunk stopped and looked around. The Weasels hid themselves under some fallen leaves. "I bid you good-morning," said the Skunk, looking toward the place where they were. "I hope you are not *too* tired. This walk has been very easy for me, but I fear it was rather long for Weasels. Besides, I have found plenty to eat and have chosen smooth paths for myself. Good-morning! I have enjoyed your company!"

When even the tip of his tail was hidden in the hole, the Weasels crawled from under the leaves and looked at each other.

"We believe he knew all the time that we were following him," they said. "He acted queerly just to fool us. The wretch!"

Yet after all, you see, he had done only what he did every night, and it was because they were watching and talking about him that they thought him going on some strange errand.

# THE THRIFTY DEER MOUSE

WHEN the days grew short and chilly, and bleak winds blew out of the great blue-gray cloud banks in the west, many of the forest people went to sleep for the winter. And not only they, but over in the meadow the Tree Frog and the Garter Snake had already crawled out of sight and were dreaming sweetly. The song birds had long before this started south, and the banks of the pond and its bottom of comfortable soft mud held many sleepers. Under the water the Frogs had snuggled down in groups out of sight. Some of the Turtles were there also, and some were in the bank.

The Ground Hogs had grown stupid and dozy before the last leaves fluttered to the ground, and had been the first of the fur-bearers to go to bed for the winter. There were so many interesting things to see and do in the late fall days that they tried exceedingly hard to keep awake.

A Weasel was telling a Ground Hog something one day—and it was a very interesting piece of gossip, only it was rather unkind, and so might better not be told here—when he saw the Ground Hog winking very slow and sleepy winks and letting his head droop lower and lower. Once he asked him if he understood. The Ground Hog jumped and opened his eyes very wide indeed, and said: "Oh, yes, yes! Perfectly! Oh-ah-ah-ah-ah-ah." His yawn didn't look so big as it sounds, because his mouth was so small.

He tried to act politely interested, but just as the Weasel reached the most exciting part of his story, the Ground Hog rolled over sound asleep. The next day he said "good-by" to his friends, wished them a happy winter, and said he might see some of them before spring, as he should come out once to make the weather. "I only hope I shall awaken in time," he said, "but I am fat enough to sleep until the violets are up."

He had to be fat, you know, to last him through the cold weather without eating. He was so stout that he could hardly waddle, his big, loose-skinned body dragged when he walked, and was even shakier than ever. He really couldn't hurry by jumping and he was so short of breath that he could barely whistle when he went into his hole.

The Raccoons went after the Ground Hog and the Skunks were later still. They never slept so very long, and said they didn't really need to at all, and wouldn't except that they had nothing to do and it made housekeeping easier. It saved so much not to have to go out to their meals in the coldest weather.

When the large people were safely out of the way, the smaller ones had their best times. The Muskrats were awake, but they had their big houses to eat and were not likely to trouble Mice and Squirrels. There was not much to fear except Owls and Weasels. The Ground Hogs had once tried to get the Great Horned Owl to go south when the Cranes did, and he had laughed in their faces. "To-whoo!" said he. "Not I! I'm not afraid of cold weather. You don't know how warm feathers are. I never wear anything else. Furs are all right, but they are not feathers."

He and his relatives sat all day in their holes, and seldom flew out except at night. Sometimes, when the day was not too bright, they made short trips out for luncheon. It was very unfortunate for any Mouse to be near at those times.

Now the snow had fallen and the beautiful still cold days had come. The Weasels' fur had changed from brown to white, as it does in cold countries in winter. The Chipmunks had taken their last scamper until early spring, and were living, each alone, in their comfortable burrows. They were most independent and thrifty. No one ever heard of a Chipmunk lacking food unless some robber had carried off his nuts and corn. The Mice think that it must be very dull for a Chipmunk to stay by himself all winter, since he does not sleep steadily. The Chipmunks do not find it so. One of them said: "Dull? I never find it dull. When I am awake, I eat or clean my fur or think. If I had any one staying with me he might rouse me when I want to sleep, or pick

THE MICE MAKE WINTER THEIR PLAYTIME.

the nut that I want for myself, or talk when I am thinking. No, thank you, I will go calling when I want company."

The Mice make winter their playtime. Then the last summer's babies are all grown up and able to look out for themselves, and the fathers and mothers have a chance to rest. The Meadow Mice come together in big parties and build groups of snug winter homes under the snow of the meadow, with many tiny covered walks leading from one to another. Their food is all around them—grass roots and brown seeds—and there is so much of it that they never quarrel to see who shall have this root and who shall have that. They sleep during the daytime and awaken to eat and visit and have a good time at night.

Sometimes they are awakened in the daytime, as they were when the Grouse broke through the snow near them. That was an accident, and the Grouse felt very sorry about it. They had snuggled down in a cozy family party near by, and were just starting out for a stroll one morning when the eldest son stumbled and fell and crushed through the snow into the little settlement of Meadow Mice.

The young Grouse was much ashamed of his awkwardness. "I am so sorry," he said. "I'm not used to my snow-shoes yet. This is the first winter I have worn them."

"That is all right," said the Oldest Mouse politely. "It must be hard to manage them at first. We hope you will have better luck after this." Then they bowed to each other and the Grouse walked off to join his brothers and sisters, lifting his feet with their newly grown feather snow-shoes very high at every step. The Meadow Mice went to work to make their homes neat again, yet they never looked really right until that snow had melted and more had fallen. One might think that the Meadow Mice and the Grouse would care less for each other after that, but it was not so. It never is so if people who make trouble are quick to say that they are sorry, and those who were hurt will keep patient and forgiving.

It was only the night after this happened that one of the Deer Mice had a great fright. His home was in a Bee tree in the forest. The Bees and he had always been the best of friends, and now that they were keeping close to their honeycomb all winter, the Deer Mouse had taken a small room in the same tree. It helped to keep him warm when he slept close to the Bees, for there was always some heat coming from their bodies. Once in a while, too, he took a nibble of honey, and they did not mind.

The Deer Mouse did not keep much of his own winter food where he lived. He had a few beechnuts near by, and when the weather was very stormy indeed he ate some of these. There was room for many more in the storeroom (another hole in the Bee tree), but he liked to keep food in many places. "It is wiser," said he. "Supposing I had them all here and this tree should be blown down, and it should fall in such a way that I couldn't reach the hole. What would I do then?"

133

He was talking to a Rabbit when he said this. The Rabbit never stored up food himself, yet he sometimes told other people how he thought it should be done. He was sure it would be better to have all the nuts in one place as the Chipmunks did. And now that the Deer Mouse had given his reasons, he was just as sure as ever. "The Bee tree is not very likely to blow down in that way," said he. "There is not much danger."

"Not much, but some," answered the Deer Mouse. "Hollow trees fall more quickly than solid ones. You may store up your food where you please and I'll take care of mine."

The Deer Mouse spoke very decidedly, although he was perfectly polite. His beautiful brown eyes looked squarely at the Rabbit, and you could tell by the position of his slender long tail that he was much in earnest. The Rabbit went home.

The Deer Mouse put away hundreds and hundreds of beechnuts. These he took carefully out of their shells and laid in nicely lined holes in tree-trunks. He used leaves for lining these places. Besides keeping food in the trees, he hid little piles of nuts under stones and logs, and tucked seeds into chinks of fences or tiny pockets in the ground. He had worked in the wheatfield after the grain was cut, picking up and carrying away the stray kernels which had fallen from the sheaves. He never counted the places where food was stored, but he was happy in thinking about them. When he lay down to sleep in the morning he always knew where the next night's meals were coming from. There was not a thriftier, happier person in the forest. He was gentle, good-natured, and exceedingly businesslike. He was also very handsome, with large ears and white belly and feet.

The night after his cousins, the Meadow Mice, had been so frightened by the Grouse, this Deer Mouse started out for a good time. He called on the Meadow Mice, ate a chestnut which he dug up in the edge of the forest, scampered up a fence-post and tasted of his hidden wheat to be sure that it was keeping well, and then went to the tree where most of his beechnuts were stored. He was not quite certain that he wanted to eat one, but he wished to be sure that they were all right before he went on. He had been invited to a party by some other Deer Mice, and so, you see, it wouldn't do for him to spoil his appetite. They would be sure to have refreshments at the party.

"I suppose they are all right," said he, as he started to run up the tree; "still it is just as well to be sure."

"My whiskers!" he exclaimed, when he reached the hole. "If that isn't just like a Red Squirrel!"

The opening into the tree had been barely large enough for him to squeeze through, and now he could pass in without crushing his fur. Around the edge of it were many marks of sharp teeth. Somebody had wanted to get in and had not found the doorway large enough. The Deer Mouse went inside and sat on his beechnuts. Then he thought and thought and thought. He knew very well that it was a Red Squirrel, for the Red Squirrels are not so thrifty as most of the nut-eaters. They make a great fuss about gathering food in the fall, and frisk and chatter and scold if anybody else comes where they are busy. For all that, the Chipmunks and the Deer Mice work much harder than they. It is not always the person who makes the greatest fuss, you know, who does the most.

A Red Squirrel is usually out of food long before spring comes, and after that he takes whatever he can lay his paws on. Sometimes the Chipmunks tell them that they should be ashamed of themselves and work harder. Then the Red Squirrels sigh and answer, "Oh, that is all very well for you to say, still you must remember that we have not such cheek pouches as you."

The Deer Mouse thought of these things. "Cheek pouches!" cried he. "I have no cheek pouches, but I lay up my own food. It is only an excuse when they say that. I don't think much of people who make excuses."

He passed through the doorway several times to see just how big it was. He found it was not yet large enough for a Red Squirrel. Then he scampered over the snow to a friend's house. "I'm not going to the party," said he. "I have some work to do."

"Work?" said the friend. "Work? In winter?" But before he had finished speaking his caller had gone.

All night long the Deer Mouse carried beechnuts from the old hiding-place to a new one. He wore quite a path in the snow between one tree and the other. His feet were tiny, but there were four of them, and his long tail dragged after him. It was not far that he had to go. The new place was one which he had looked at before. It was in a maple tree, and had a long and very narrow opening leading to the storeroom. It was having to go so far into the tree that had kept the Deer Mouse from using it before. Now he liked it all the better for having this.

"If that Red Squirrel ever gnaws his way in here," he said, "he won't have any teeth left for eating."

When the sun rose, the Deer Mouse went to sleep in the maple tree. The Red Squirrel came and gnawed at the opening into his old storeroom. If he had gnawed all day he would surely have gotten in. As it was, he had to spend much time hunting for food. He found some frozen apples still hanging in the orchard, and bit away at them until he reached the seeds inside. He found one large acorn, but it was old and tasted musty. He also squabbled with another Red Squirrel and chased him nearly to the farmyard. Then Collie heard them and chased him most of the way back.

When night came and he ran off to sleep in his hollow tree, he had made the hole almost, but not quite, large enough. He could smell the beechnuts inside, and it made him hungry to think how good they would taste. "I will get up early to-morrow morning and come here," he said. "I can gnaw my way in before breakfast, and then!"

He went off in fine leaps to his home and was soon sound asleep. In summer he often frolicked around half of the night, but now it was cold, and when the sun went down he liked to get home quickly and wrap up warmly in his tail. The Red Squirrel was hardly out of sight when the Deer Mouse came along his path in the snow and up to his old storeroom. His dainty white feet shook a little as he climbed, and he hardly dared look in for fear of finding the hole empty. You can guess how happy he was to find everything safe.

All night long he worked, and when morning came it was a very tired little Deer Mouse who carried his last beechnut over the trodden path to its safe new resting place. He was tired but he was happy.

There was just one other thing that he wanted to do. He wanted to see that Red Squirrel when he found the beechnuts gone. He waited near by for him to come. It was a beautiful, still winter morning when the hoar-frost clung to all the branches, and the shadows which fell upon the snow looked fairly blue, it was so cold. The Deer Mouse crouched down upon his dainty feet to keep them warm, and wrapped his tail carefully around to help.

Along came the Red Squirrel, dashing finely and not noticing the Deer Mouse at all. A few leaps brought him to the tree, a quick run took him to the hole, and then he began to gnaw. The Deer Mouse was growing sleepy and decided not to wait any longer. He ran along near the Red Squirrel. "Oh, good-morning!" said he. "Beautiful day! I see you are getting that hole ready to use. Hope you will like it. I liked it very well for a while, but I began to fear it wasn't safe."

"Wh-what do you mean?" asked the Red Squirrel sternly. He had seen the Deer Mouse's eyes twinkle and he was afraid of a joke.

"Oh," answered the Deer Mouse with a careless whisk of his tail, "I had some beechnuts there until I moved them."

"You had!" exclaimed the Red Squirrel. He did not gnaw any after that. He suddenly became very friendly. "You couldn't tell me where to find food, I suppose," said he. "I'd eat almost anything."

The Deer Mouse thought for a minute. "I believe," said he, "that you will find plenty in the farmer's barn, but you must look out for the Dog."

"Thank you," said the Red Squirrel. "I will go."

"There!" said the Deer Mouse after he had whisked out of sight. "He has gone to steal from the farmer. Still, men have so very much that they ought to share with Squirrels."

And that, you know, is true.

# THE HUMMING-BIRD AND THE HAWK-MOTH

T HE Hawk-Moths are acquainted with nearly everybody and are great society people. They are invited to companies given by the daylight set, and also to parties given at night by those who sleep during the day. This is not because the Hawk-Moths are always awake. Oh dear, no! There is nobody in pond, forest, meadow, marsh, or even in houses, who can be well and strong and happy without plenty of sleep.

The Hawk-Moths were awake more or less during the day, but it was not until the sun was low in the western sky that they were busiest. When every tree had a shadow two or three times as long as the tree itself, then one heard the whir-r-r of wings and the Hawk-Moths darted past. They staid up long after the daylight people went to bed. The Catbird, who sang from the tip of the topmost maple tree branch long after most of his birds friends were asleep, said that when he tucked his head under his wing the Hawk-Moths were still flying. In that way, of course, they became acquainted with the people of the night-time.

There was one fine large Hawk-Moth who used to be a Tomato Worm when he was young, although he really fed as much upon potato vines as upon tomato plants. He was handsome from the tip of his long, slender sucking-tongue to the tip of his trim, gray body. His wings were pointed and light gray in color, with four blackish lines across the hind ones. His body was also gray, and over it and his wings were many dainty markings of black or very dark gray. On the back part of it he had ten square yellow spots edged with black. There were also twenty tiny white spots there, but he did not care so much for them. He always felt badly to think that his yellow spots showed so little. That couldn't be helped, of course, and he should have been thankful to have them at all.

Another thing which troubled him was the fact that he couldn't see his own yellow spots. He would have given a great deal to do so. He could see the yellow spots of other Hawk-Moths who had been Tomato Worms when he was, but that was not like seeing his own. He had tried and tried, and it always ended in the same way—his eyes were tired and his back ached. His body was so much stouter and stiffer than that of his butterfly cousins that he could not bend it easily.

When he got to thinking about his yellow spots he often flew away to the farmer's potato-fields, where the young Tomato Worms were feeding. He would fly around them and cry out: "Look at my yellow spots. Are they not fine?" Then he would dart away to the vegetable-garden and balance himself in the air over the tomato plants. The humming of his wings would make the Tomato Worms there look up, and he would say: "If you are good little Worms and eat a great deal, you may some day become fine Moths like me and have ten yellow spots apiece."

Sometimes he even went down to the corner where the farmer had tobacco plants growing, and showed his yellow spots to the Tomato Worms there. He never went anywhere else, for these worms do not care for other things to eat. Everywhere that he went the Tomato Worms exclaimed: "Oh! Oh! What beautiful yellow spots! What wonderful yellow spots!" When he flew away they would not eat for a while, but rested on their fat pro-legs, raised the front part of their bodies in the air, folded their six little real legs under their chins, and thought and thought and thought. They always sat in that position when they were thinking, and they had a great many cousins who did the same thing. It was a habit which ran in the family.

When other people saw them sitting in this way, with their real legs crossed under their chins, they always cried: "Look at the Sphinxes!" although not one of them knew what a Sphinx really was. And that was just one of their habits. This was why the Hawk-Moths were sometimes called Sphinx-Moths.

It was not kind in the Hawk-Moth to come and make the Tomato Worms discontented. If he had stayed away, they would have thought it the loveliest thing in the world to be fat green Tomato Worms with two sorts of legs and each with a horn standing up on the hind end of his body. That is not the usual place for horns, still it does very well, and these horns are worn only for looks. They are never used for poking or stinging.

Before the Hawk-Moth came to visit them, the Tomato Worms had thought it would be quiet, and restful, and pleasant to lie all winter in their shining brown pupa-cases in the ground, waiting for the spring to finish turning them into Moths. Now they were so impatient to get their yellow spots that they could hardly bear the idea of waiting. They did not even care about the long, slender tongue-case which every Tomato-Worm has on his pupa-case, and which looks like a handle to it.

One day the Tomato Worms told the Ruby-throated Humming-Bird about all this. The Humming-Bird was a very sensible fellow, and would no doubt have been a hard-working husband and father if his wife had not been so independent. He had been a most devoted lover, and helped build a charming nest of fern-wool and plant-down, and cover it with beautiful gray-green lichens. When done it was about as large as half of a hen's egg, and a morning-glory blossom would have more than covered it. The lichens were just the color of the branch on which it rested, and one could hardly see where it was. That is the nicest thing to be said about a nest. If a bird ever asks you what you think of his nest, and you wish to say something particularly agreeable, you must stare at the tree and ask: "Where is it?" Then, when he has shown it to you, you may speak of the soft lining, or the fine weaving, or the stout way in which it is fastened to the branches.

After this nest was finished and the two tiny white eggs laid in it, Mrs. Humming-Bird cared for nothing else. She would not go honey-hunting with her husband, or play in the air with him as she used to do. He tried to coax her by darting down toward her as she sat covering her eggs, and by squeaking the sweetest things he could think of into her ear, but she acted as though she cared more for the eggs than for him, and did not even squeak sweet things back. So, of course, he went away, and let her hatch and bring up her children as she chose. It was certainly her fault that he left her. She might not have been able to leave the eggs, but she could have squeaked.

Now that the Ruby-throated Humming-Bird had no home cares, he made many calls on his friends. They were very short calls, for he would seldom sit down, yet he heard and told much news while he balanced himself in the air with his tiny feet curled up and his wings moving so fast that one could not see them.

When the Tomato Worms told him how they felt about the Hawk-Moth's yellow spots, he became very indignant. "Those poor young worms!" he said to himself. "It is a shame, and something must be done about it."

The more he thought, the angrier he became, and his feathers fairly stood on end. He hardly knew what he was doing, and ran his long, slender bill into the same flowers several times, although he had taken all the honey from them at first.

That night, when the sun had set and the silvery moon was peeping above a violet-colored cloud in the eastern sky, the Ruby-throated Humming-Bird sat on the tip of a spruce-tree branch and waited for the Hawk-Moth.

"I hope nobody else will hear me talking," said he. "It would sound so silly if I were overheard." He sat very still, his tiny feet clutching the branch tightly. It was late twilight now and really time that he should go to sleep, but he had decided that if he could possibly keep awake he would teach the Hawk-Moth a lesson.

"I wish he would hurry," said he. "I can hardly keep my eyes open." He did not yawn because he had not the right kind of mouth for it. You know a yawn ought to be nearly round. His beak would have made one a great, great many times higher than it was wide, and that would have been exceedingly unbecoming to him.

Yellow evening primroses grew near the spruce-tree, and the tall stalks were opening their flowers for the night. Above the seed-pods and below the buds on each stalk two, three, or four blossoms were slowly unfolding. The Ruby-throated

Humming-Bird did not often stay up long enough to see this, and he watched the four smooth yellow petals of one untwist themselves until they were free to spring wide open. He had watched five blossoms when he heard the Hawk-Moth coming. Then he darted toward the primroses and balanced himself daintily before one while he sucked honey from it.

Whir-r-r-r! The Hawk-Moth was there. "Good evening," said he. "Rather late for you, isn't it?"

"It is a little," answered the Humming-Bird. "Growing a bit chilly, too, isn't it? I should think you'd be cold without feathers. Mine are such a comfort. Feel as good as they look, and that is saying a great deal."

The Hawk-Moth balanced himself before another primrose and seemed to care more about sucking honey up his long tongue-tube than he did about talking.

"I think it is a great thing to have a touch of bright color, too," said the Humming-Bird. "The beautiful red spot on my throat looks particularly warm and becoming when the weather is cool. You ought to have something of the sort."

"I have yellow spots—ten of them," answered the Hawk-Moth sulkily.

"You have?" exclaimed the Humming-Bird in the most surprised way. "Oh yes! I think I do remember something about them. It is a pity they

THE HUMMING-BIRD AND THE HAWK-MOTH.

don't show more. Mrs. Humming-Bird never wears bright colors. She says it would not do. People would see her on her nest if she did. Excepting the red spot, she is dressed like me—white breast, green back and head, and black wings and tail. Green is another good color. You should wear something green.

The Hawk-Moth murmured that he didn't see any particular use in wearing green.

"Oh," said the Humming-Bird, "it is just the thing to wear—neat, never looks dusty" (here the Hawk-Moth drew back, for his own wings, you know, were almost dust color), "and matches the leaves perfectly."

The Hawk-Moth said something about having to go and thinking that the primrose honey was not so good as usual.

"I thought it excellent," said the Humming-Bird. "Perhaps you do not get it so easily as I. Ah yes, you use a tongue-tube. What different ways different people do have. Now I like honey, but I could not live many days on that alone. What I care most for is the tiny insects that I find eating it. And you cannot eat meat. What a pity! I must say that you seem to make the best of it, though, and do fairly well. Oh, must you go? Well, good night."

The Hawk-Moth flew away feeling very much disgusted. He had always thought himself the most beautiful person in the neighborhood. He rather thought so still. Yet it troubled him to know that others did not think so, and he began to remember how many times he had heard people admire the Ruby-throated Humming-Bird. He never liked him after that. But neither did he brag.

The young Tomato Worms soon forgot what the Hawk-Moth had said to them, and became happy and contented once more. The Ruby-throated Humming-Bird never cared to talk about it, yet he was once heard to say that he would rather offend the Hawk-Moth and even make him a little unhappy than to have him bothering the poor little Tomato Worms all the time.